C000152311

100 WALKS IN
Wiltshire

The Crowood Press

First published in 1990 by
The Crowood Press
Ramsbury, Marlborough
Wiltshire SN8 2HR

Revised edition 1997

British Library Cataloguing in Publication Data

A catalogue record for this book is available from the British Library

ISBN 1 86126 060 1

Maps by Philip Smith and Allan Williams

Typeset by Carreg Limited, Ross-on-Wye, Herefordshire

Printed in Great Britain by J W Arrowsmith Ltd, Bristol

THE CONTRIBUTORS

Naomi Ashton

Bill Barker

Rosie Booton & Guy Hankin

Norman Buckley

Linda Emsley

Sally Hussey

Tess Lecomber

Les Maple

Ray Skinner

Lynda Thompson

Colin Tovey

Andrea West

Mary Wheeler

CONTENTS

North-West

71. All Cannings and Stanton St Bernard 8m (13km)
72. Barbury Castle 7m (14.5km)
73. and shorter versions
74. Aldbourne 10m (16km)
75. and shorter versions
76. Chiseldon $10^1/_2$m (17km)
77. and shorter version 7m (11km)
78. Pewsey Wharf to Knap Hill $10^1/_2$m (17km)

South-West

79. Sherrington and Boyton Down 4m (6.5km)
80. Around Tollard Royal $4^1/_2$m (7.5km)
81. Gasper Mill 5m (8km)
82. Salisbury Plain and the Lavingtons 5m (8km)
83. Foxholes 5m (8km)
84. Wardour Woods and Castle $5^1/_2$m (9km)
85. Whitesheet Hill $6^1/_2$m (10.5km)
86. Bidcombe Down $6^1/_2$m (10.5km)
87. North Bradley and West Ashton $6^3/_4$m (11km)
88. Bratton and Edington $6^3/_4$m (11km)
89. Shaston Drove 7m (11km)
90. Middle Hill 7m (11km)
91. Broad Chalke and the Ebble Valley $7^1/_2$m (12km)
92. Around Sutton Veny 10m (16km)
93. Kingston Deverill 10m (16km)

South-East

94. The Winterbournes 3m (5km)
95. Near the River Avon 4m (6.5km)
96. Chute Causeway $4^1/_2$m (7.5km)
97. Ludgershall Castle 5m (8km)
98. Old Sarum and Lower Woodford 5m (8km)
99. Upavon and North Newnton 7m (11km)
100. Great Wishford $7^1/_2$m (12km)

PUBLISHER'S NOTE

We very much hope that you enjoy the routes presented in this book, which has been compiled with the aim of allowing you to explore the area in the best possible way - on foot.

We strongly recommend that you take the relevant map for the area, and for this reason we list the appropriate Ordnance Survey maps for each route. Whilst the details and descriptions given for each walk were accurate at time of writing, the countryside is constantly changing, and a map will be essential if, for any reason, you are unable to follow the given route. It is good practice to carry a map and use it so that you are always aware of your exact location.

We cannot be held responsible if some of the details in the route descriptions are found to be inaccurate, but should be grateful if walkers would advise us of any major alterations. Please note that whenever you are walking in the countryside you are on somebody else's land, and we must stress that you should *always* keep to established rights of way, and *never* cross fences, hedges or other boundaries unless there is a clear crossing point.

Remember the country code:

Enjoy the country and respect its life and work
Guard against all risk of fire
Fasten all gates
Keep dogs under close control
Keep to public footpaths across all farmland
Use gates and stiles to cross field boundaries
Leave all livestock, machinery and crops alone
Take your litter home
Help to keep all water clean
Protect wildlife, plants and trees
Make no unnecessary noise

The walks are listed by length - from approximately 1 to 12 miles - but the amount of time taken will depend on the fitness of the walkers and the time spent exploring any points of interest along the way. Nearly all the walks are circular and most offer recommendations for refreshments.

Good walking.

NOTE

It will be seen by just a glance at the map that there seems to be a dearth of walks described in the southern half of the county. This is due to the presence of Salisbury Plain and the activities of the Ministry of Defence which do not, on the whole, co-exist well with the leisure walker.

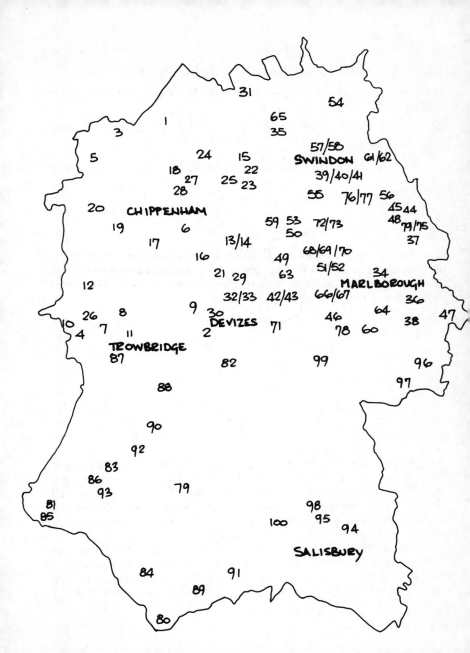

Maps: OS Sheets Landranger 173; Pathfinder ST 88/98.

*A gentle stroll along the picturesque streets and watermeadows
of England's oldest borough.*

Start: The car park in Cross Hayes (a large square) near the town
hall, Malmesbury.

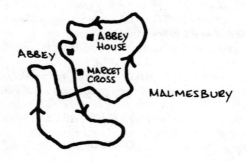

With your back to the town hall, take the road leaving the far left corner of the square. This is Silver Street, so called because it once contained Malmesbury's mint. Go down Silver Street, after a few yards the road gives way to gentle steps, until you reach the bottom of the hill, whereupon you turn left past the bowling-green. At the edge of the green, turn left again, down a gravel footpath. This will take you firstly over a sluice-cum-footbridge and then over a stile into watermeadows.

After a further hundred yards or so, by an old derelict railway line, you will come to another stile. Go over this, keeping between the two courses of the River Avon (Tetbury Branch – alternatively known as the River Ingleburn). Eventually you reach a stile by a road, which you should cross, taking the path immediately in front of the pub car park. Continue along this path, with the river on your left, until, after 200 yards or so, the imposing facade of **Abbey House** looms above you. The abbey, too, soon comes into sight.

At the next road, turn left over the river and up some steps in front of you, bearing left as soon as you begin to climb. This leads to the remarkable **Malmesbury Abbey** and cloister gardens which you will want to explore in detail. Equally interesting is the picturesque wisteria-clad hotel called **The Old Bell**.

Leave the abbey through the south door and go towards the **Tolsey**, or gatehouse, directly in front of you. About $^2/_3$ of the way you may wish to search for the intriguing gravestone to the memory of Hannah Twynnoy. Go through the Tolsey and, passing the old **Market Cross**, head down the **High Street**. Continue in this direction, bearing left downhill into Lower High Street, from where a fine view of the **Almshouses** can be appreciated.

Join the pavement on the right of the road and just before St John's Bridge go through a gateway on the right and then turn left over a footbridge above the Avon. As you cross the footbridge, you will see the town's silk mills, recently converted into flats, to your left. Walk a few yards along the road before turning right through a gate into the watermeadow. Keeping the river on your right proceed along the path until the impressive **King's House** comes into view standing high on the escarpment above the river.

After about 600 yards – having only briefly left the bank of the river – you cross a small footbridge over a stream. Turn to the right and then go over a second and larger footbridge, with a road sign marked 'Burnivale' facing you. Bear right up the path between two stone walls until it turns into a very narrow street. Take a little alleyway with railings, on the left opposite a lamp-post, and follow this until you reach the High Street. In front of you and slightly to your left is St Dennis Road. Follow this to **Cross Hayes** and the start.

POINTS OF INTEREST:

Malmesbury claims to be the oldest borough in England having been granted a charter by Alfred the Great in 880AD. King Ethelstan, who is buried in the Abbey, later gave land to the town after its menfolk had helped him defeat Norse invaders. This land is still known as King's Heath.

Virtually every building in Malmesbury has its own special Points of Interest and is worth a moment of your time. Here we consider only those that, in the opinion of the author, are quite outstanding.

Abbey House – This fine building was erected in the 16th century after William Stumpe had bought the abbey and its lands after the Dissolution of the Monasteries in the time of Henry VIII. He paid only £1516 for the entire Abbey property. William Stumpe was a wealthy, local clothier who set up his factory inside the Abbey itself, though two years later he gave the nave to the town for use as a church. Abbey House is now a nunnery.

Malmesbury Abbey – The first abbey was founded by St.Aldhelm in the 7th century, though what we now see was mainly built in the 12th century. Restoration work was carried out in the 14th century when a mighty tower was added, standing some 445 feet high. This collapsed in the 15th century, destroying much of the eastern end of the church, but nevertheless the abbey is still one of the finest examples of Norman ecclesiastical architecture anywhere in the country. Notice particularly the magnificent 12th-century carved porch, the tomb of King Ethelstan, the first Saxon king to rule the whole of England, who died in 940AD, and the mysterious little watching loft on the south wall. When the Parvise is open, some fascinating manuscripts, coins and documents are on view.

In the 11th century a monk at the Abbey, one Elmer, jumped off the tower wearing home-made wings in the vain belief that he had discovered the secret of man-powered flight. One story has him gliding over 200 yards before he crashed. He broke both his legs and was crippled for the rest of his life. Elmer's flight is today commemorated in a stained glass window.

The Old Bell – It is believed that the inn may well have once been part of a Saxon castle which is known to have been demolished in 1216. Since the site was then used for the Abbey guesthouse part of the inn's walls are thought to be from that building.

Tolsey – This gatehouse guards the entrance to the abbey grounds and was possibly the town lock-up. The Apostle's Spoon, on the left as you leave the abbey, is the oldest private house in the town.

Market Cross – Nearly 500 years old, the market cross was built, it is recorded, for poor market folks to stand dry when rain cometh!

High Street – The street once contained many public houses, almost all of which have now changed their use. The exception is the King's Arms Hotel, reached via an archway into a courtyard. On the opposite side, The George Veterinary Hospital was once an 18th-century coaching inn.

Almshouses – A hospital was first founded on this site in the late 13th century by the Order of St John of Jerusalem. At the Dissolution of the Monasteries, the Order was banished and the buildings were later bought by the Capital Burgesses, who donated £10 a year for the provision of almshouses on the site. The old archway is all that remains from the original hospital building. The inscription above it records the Burgesses' gift of £10.

King's House – This fine stone building dates from the 1670s. Despite the name, there is no regal connection, this having been the home of a Mr King, a local clothier. The western portion of the house was probably used originally as a weaving shed.

Cross Hayes – The word Hayes means common and this area was the market place for the town from Saxon times until quite recently. At Queen Victoria's Jubilee the area was turned into an outdoor dining room for the whole town.

REFRESHMENTS:
Too numerous to mention.

Walk 2   DREWS POND AND POTTERNE WOODS   3¹/₄m (5km)

Maps: OS Sheets Landranger 173; Pathfinder ST 85/95 and SU 05/15.

A short, pleasant ramble on elevated ground.

Start: At 999592, lay-by on the Devizes to Potterne road.

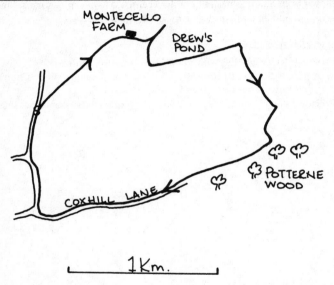

Take the broad track from the Devizes end of the lay-by, signposted 'Drews Pond Lane 1'. On reaching Montecello farmhouse look out for a disc 'footpath' sign on the right and cross into a field, following an obvious path along the edge. Shortly after entering woodland a junction is reached. Our route is to the right, but a short detour to the left drops down to Drews Pond, a charming small lake which, unfortunately, lacks a really good viewpoint accessible to the public.

Returning to the route, the path climbs steadily along the edge of a field. On emerging from a wooded section, there is a gap in the fence on the left. Take this and carry on for about ¹/₂ mile on elevated ground with unusual views of Devizes across a wooded valley, Roundway hospital being prominent.

On reaching a broad cart-track turn right and at a junction turn right again to reach

Potterne Woods. Turn right yet again and follow a good track along the edge of the woodland. Meandering tracks among the trees can be used as attractive alternatives, with occasional long views to Salisbury Plain. At a meeting of several trackways bear gently right. This is Coxhill Lane which descends through a surprisingly deep and leafy cutting towards **Potterne**. At the first road junction swing right then left into a path protected by bollards. This by-passes the village centre, reaching the main road close to the general store. The lay-by is $^1/_3$ mile further. To view Porch House and the church carry on to the junction of Coxhill Lane and the main road and turn right.

POINTS OF INTEREST:
Potterne – Large village with good Early English church. Porch House is a well preserved half-timbered 15th-century building on the main street. Church House, by the church gates, dates from 1614.
Potterne Woods – Attractive mixed woodland along the side and crest of a steep scarp.

REFRESHMENTS:
The Bell Inn (tel no: 0380 3067).

Walk 3   PINKNEY TO EASTON GREY   3½m (6km)

Maps: OS Sheets Landranger 173; Pathfinder ST 88/98.

A short, pleasant walk through Wiltshire farmland.

Start: At 866869, the Eagle Inn, Pinkney.

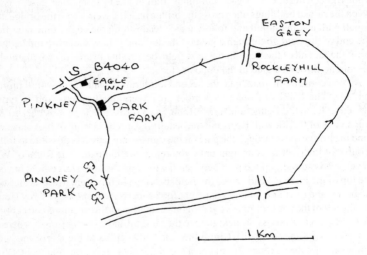

The Eagle Inn lies beside the B4040 (Sherston to Malmesbury road), on the south side, just a short way past the entrance to Pinkney Park. If you use the inn car park, please check with the landlord beforehand.

With your back to the inn, turn left along the verge of the B4040, then, after a few yards, left again along a road signed as a no through road and as unsuitable for long vehicles. Follow this road to Park Farm, Now take the track leading up the hill away from the farm. Proceed for about ½ mile, always keeping the dry stone wall of the estate on your right until you reach the second large gateway in the estate wall. Then bear left towards the metal gate in the hedge in front of you and turn left at the road.

Keep to the road, passing one house on your left and at the crossroads, about 1 mile further on, go straight on until, a short distance further on, you see a signpost marked

'By-way' on your right. Take the track to the left which is, in fact, the ancient **Fosse Way** and continue into a field. Here you leave the Fosse Way and follow the grassy track veering off to the left. This beautiful stretch of countryside, close to the River Avon, is the site of an ancient Roman settlement, though not a trace of it can be seen.

As you reach the next gate, look back and right for a fine view of Whatley Manor, now an hotel. Pass through the gate and follow the track ahead, keeping to the hedge on your right. After the next gate, continue straight ahead to another gate, passing between the ruined buildings, then cross the bridge near the weir. From the bridge, take the small path leading uphill and follow it as it leads along the edge of the next field. At the end of the field go through a gate on the left and follow the left-hand hedge to a gate at the far end of the field. In the next field, bear right towards the small, modern house and go through a gate in the opposite fence.

As you come to the road, take the second left turning, walking downhill through the village. The houses of this tiny hamlet are exceptionally pretty and in typical Cotswold style. At the T-junction, turn left and, as you cross the river, look back to your left for a view of Ruckleyhill Farm and the beautiful gardens in front of it. A short way beyond the bridge, pass through the gate on the right. From here it is possible to follow the course of the river to your right until you rejoin the footpath. The Right of Way, however, leads straight up the path between the trees and into the large field beyond. At the top of the incline, head across the field, bearing slightly right towards the small copse beside the river and look to your right for a superb view of Easton Grey House. Just to the left of the copse climb two sets of fence rails beside horse jumps and continue in the same direction across the next field to the far right-hand corner (this is where the river walk rejoins the footpath). Climb the stile and keeping to the left of the hedge continue through the next field, until you a see a stile in the fence on your right. Climb this into the adjacent field, continuing in the same direction, and when the field opens out to your left, bear left towards the small path leading between the farm buildings. Walk through the farmyard, then turn right to revere the outward route back to the start point.

POINTS OF INTEREST:
Fosse Way – This Roman road ran from Lincoln to Exeter and is so named because it was bordered on both sides by a 'fosse' or ditch.

REFRESHMENTS:
The Eagle Inn, at the start.
The Carpenters Arms, Sherston.
The Rattlebone, Sherston.

Walk 4 WESTWOOD AND FARLEIGH HUNGERFORD 4m (6.5km)

Maps: OS Sheets Landranger 173; Pathfinder ST 85/95.

A lovely and exhilarating walk across open countryside, visiting an old castle.

Start: At 812590, the National Trust car park at Westwood Manor.

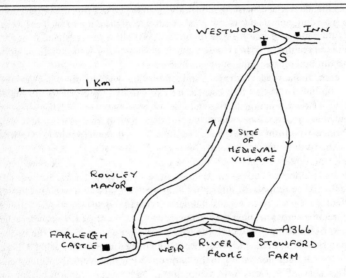

Leave the car park and turn left along the road for 20 yards. Now turn left over a barred stile and head across the field beyond in the direction of the finger-post pointing to Stowford. At the far side, go to the left of a small pond, then through a gate/gap and maintain direction across the next field. Cross a stile and continue. There are good views from here: if it is clear you may be able to see the Westbury White Horse in the distance. At the far side of the field, go over a barred stile to the left of a gate, and bear slightly right down the next field, aiming towards the left-hand corner of a hedge coming in from the right. Continue down the field to reach a gap in the low hedge ahead. Go through and bear left along a farm track. The track crosses a small stream and then turns right. Continue along the track, with the stream on your right, to reach the A366, just opposite Stowford Farm.

Cross the road, with care, and turn right for 100 yards to reach the entrance to Stowford Forge showroom. Here, turn left along the drive for 10 yards, then turn right across a field. Although not shown on the map, there is a path which runs between the road (the A366), on the right, and the River Frome, which soon appears on the left. On this section of the walk you cross into Somerset. Soon you will be able to see the tower of **Farleigh Castle** ahead. Shortly after passing a weir on the River Frome, bear right to reach a gate in the right-hand hedge. Go through and turn left to reach a road junction. To visit the castle, turn left, go over two road bridges, and follow the road as it bends right uphill. The entrance to the castle is at the top of the hill, on the right. (For refreshment, the Hungerford Arms is further on up the road.)

From the castle, turn left and retrace your steps back to the road junction. Now, go straight ahead up a minor road, signed 'Westwood $1^1/_2$'. The road ascends fairly steeply and, at the top, you may catch glimpses of Rowley Manor through the hedgerow to your left. Continue to reach a lodge on the left. About 500 yards further on, to the right, is the site of a medieval village, though you will need a good imagination as there is very little to be seen. Continue along the road to reach Westwood Church, on the left. About 50 yards beyond the church, turn right into the car park beside **Westwood Manor**, to finish of the walk.

POINTS OF INTEREST:

Farleigh Castle – The remains of this castle sit peacefully on a hill. The first castle dates from the 14th century. It has 16th-century stained glass windows of exceptional quality, a crypt with eight lead coffins, and the tomb of Sir Thomas Hungerford who built the castle. Managed by English Heritage, the castle is open as follows: 1 April – 30 September (10am – 6pm); 1 October – 31 October (10am – 4pm); 1 November – 31 March (10am – 4pm on Wednesday to Sunday only). It is closed on Christmas Eve, Christmas Day, Boxing Day and New Year's Day.

Westwood – The Manor House (National Trust) is a lovely old house and is rich in curiosities. It dates from the 15th century and has fine Jacobean windows and topiary. The Manor, and the Church of St Mary the Virgin which stands beside it, complement each other in their quiet idyllic appearance.

REFRESHMENTS:

The Hungerford Arms, Farleigh.

The New Inn, Westwood.

Stowford Farm is open in the afternoon for cream teas, from Easter to the end of October.

Walk 5   **LUCKINGTON**   4m (6.5km)

Maps: OS Sheets Landranger 173; Pathfinder ST 88/89.
An easy walk with good views.
Start: Luckington Church.

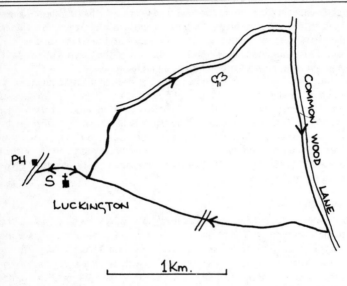

After visiting the church, leave the churchyard by a small gate on the north side. There are stables on your left. Follow the track, which bears left, over a ford. Walk up the village street to a turning on your right over a second ford. In about $^1/_2$ mile you will see **Sherston Vineyard** on the right. Follow the track for about 1 mile to a crossroads. Go straight over and carry on to the next crossroads. Turn right down Commonwood Lane and follow it for about 1 mile. It will then bend right, but you keep straight on up a grassy track – there are two large clumps of trees on your left. Opposite the end of the second clump of trees turn right through a farm gate and, keeping the hedge on your right, continue to the far corner of the field. Go over a wood bar in the hedge into the next field and, turning left, cross the field with the hedge on your left to the left-hand of two gaps in the hedge in front of you. Here carry straight on until you cross a lane and can see **Luckington Church** in front of you.

POINTS OF INTEREST:

Sherston Vineyard – Open daily except Sundays from 10.00am-5.00pm. You can taste and purchase a variety of wines and ciders and also buy garden accessories made from the old barrels.

Luckington Church – Note the little bridges between the wall and path around the church and a notice on the north wall of the tower warning you of falling masonry!

REFRESHMENTS:

The Old Royal Ship Inn, Luckington (tel no: 0666 840222). Has friendly service and good food and is open all day during August and September.

Walk 6 BREMHILL AND MAUD HEATH'S HIGHWAY 4m (6.5km)

Maps: OS Sheets Landranger 173; Pathfinder ST 87/97.

A delightful walk through rolling hills along well-marked paths.

Start: The church, Bremhill.

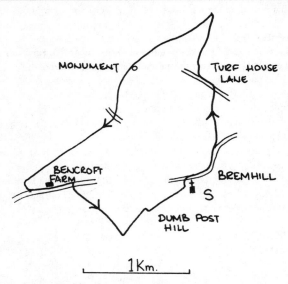

Go down the main street to the bottom of the hill. As the road begins to go uphill, go through the next gate on the left and cross the field to a gate on the opposite side. Bear right towards the brow of the right-hand hillside. Go through the gate near the telegraph pole ahead of you, and turn left at the road. Take the first turning on the right, signposted 'Charlcut', looking to the right for a good view of the downs beyond Calne. Pass some houses on the left, then about 20 yards before you reach a dilapidated wooden barn on the left, turn sharp left through a gate and into a field. Keeping the hedge on your right, cross the field to the next gate. Continue in the same direction through several more fields, always following the line of the fences and hedges, until you reach the monument to **Maud Heath**. The views from the monument and all along this stretch of the walk are superb.

From the monument, continue in the same direction as before towards the farm surrounded by pine trees. Cross the road and pass through the gateway opposite, where another inscription to Maud Heath is mounted on the stone pillar on the right. Make for the clump of trees ahead and, keeping to the left side of the wood, pass through several more fields until you reach another wood directly in front of you. Bear left just in front of the trees to the first gate on the right, from which there are fine views across the valley to Derry Hill.

Turn left at the road and pass Bencroft Farm and the bungalow beyond. Then, opposite the next metal gate on the left, a few yards further on, look for a small and well-hidden path which leads into the woodland on your right. Follow this to a gate at the end of the trees and bear left across the field keeping to the left of the wood in the middle distance. Once past the wood, bear slightly right towards the small house among the trees. Go through the gate, turn left at the road and continue up the hill, passing the Dumb Post pub on your right. This rather eccentric pub commands good views from its lounge bar and has seats outside on its pleasant front lawn. Look out for the impressive collection of Toby-jugs above the bar.

At the T-junction, cross the road and take the footpath which begins as the garage drive of the house just opposite the pub sign. Climb the stile to the left of the garage and follow the left-hand hedge to another stile. The path now leads through the grounds of a large, old house. Keep to the left of the tennis court and continue into the churchyard of **Bremhill Church** from there returning to your starting point.

POINTS OF INTEREST:
Maud Heath – Now almost part of the folklore of this area, Maud Heath lived in medieval times, and in 1474 made a bequest of land in order to build and maintain a causeway through the Avon marshes to Chippenham. Fragments of this causeway are still visible, principally at Kellaways on the Avon, where there is another monument to her. The Bremhill path was also part of her route to town.

Bremhill Church – This ancient church has some Saxon and Norman stonework and a 12th-century font. Between 1804 and 1850, the vicar here was William Bowles, who was to influence the writings of Coleridge and Southey. An inscription to an old soldier on the wall of a church, together with the lines to Maud Heath, are written by him.

REFRESHMENTS:
The Dumb Post, Bremhill (tel no: 0249 813192).

Walk 7   **BRADFORD-ON-AVON TO AVONCLIFF**   4m (6.5km)
Maps: OS Sheets Landranger 173; Pathfinder ST 86/96.
A delightful and easy walk with no steep ascents.
Start: St Margaret's car park in the centre of Bradford-on-Avon.

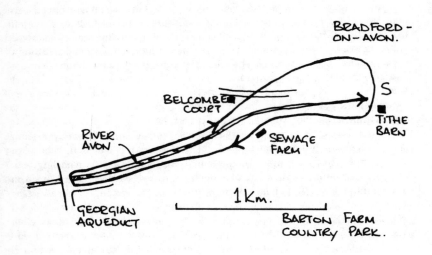

From the **Bradford-on-Avon** car park follow the signs for the swimming pool.
Continue along the river and under the railway bridge. To the right can be seen the
ancient Packhorse Bridge, and to the left a group of very fine 14th-century buildings,
one of which is the Tithe Barn. Proceed along the path which starts the country walk,
which is marked by the adjacent information board. From here there are some good
views of the old weavers' cottages on the hillside. Leaving Bradford behind, follow the
path and the gently winding river. Another information board marks the end of the
walk. Go left and walk up the slight incline, which will take you on to the **Kennet and
Avon canal** towpath. You are still following the river, but at a higher level, with far
reaching views across to Winsley (on the right) with its sloping patchwork fields and
grazing cattle. The Cross Guns pub and canal shop can be found at the end of the path
by turning right and walking down the slope. Food and drink can be consumed outside

28

whilst enjoying the spectacular weir with magnificent views of the Limpley Stoke valley, as well as the impressive Georgian Aqueduct. If cream teas are preferred the Avon Villa bed and breakfast serves homemade scones. The villa can be found by walking under the aqueduct.

To make the round trip back to Bradford-on-Avon walk over the aqueduct and follow the railway line north of the river. Turn right towards Bradford-on-Avon on to Belcombe Road (B3108). Belcombe Court, an old Georgian manor house, can be seen on the left. As the road narrows keep to the right and take the steps down to Barton Orchard – note the 18th-century weavers' houses. Continue past the chantry and at the bottom is Church Street, which houses the Norman parish church and the ancient Saxon church of St Lawrence. Keep to the right and follow the road over the bridge. You are now back in St Margaret's car park.

POINTS OF INTEREST:
Bradford-on-Avon – The Packhorse Bridge (1340) , also known as Barton Bridge, is a very good example of medieval architecture. The bridge belongs to the Barton Farm complex and has many links with the past. The Tithe Barn (1340) is an impressive cathedral-like building. Despite its gargantuan proportions it has a homely feel. Steeped in history you can almost feel the activity that once took place there. The Saxon Church (1001) is another rich treasure of the town. The carved angels that adorn the chancel act as guardians and seem content with their task. Westbury House (1700s) is a fine example of an 18th-century clothier's house and has a long history in the cloth trade, and was once the scene of a cloth workers' riot. Holy Trinity Church is largely Norman and is nicely aspected by the river, and flanked by the Saxon church and weavers' cottages. The church also boasts some examples of medieval sculpture.

REFRESHMENTS:
The Cross Guns Public House (tel no: 02216 2335). Serves food and afternoon teas. Children, walkers and dogs welcome.
Avon Villa Bed and Breakfast (tel no: 02216 3867). Afternoon teas served on the lawn. All welcome including dogs.
The Riverside Inn (tel no: 02216 3526). Sit outside and enjoy the river Avon. All welcome but dogs are to be kept outside.

Walk 8   HOLT AND GREAT CHALFIELD   4m (6.5km)

Maps: OS Sheets Landranger 173; Pathfinder ST 86/96.

A walk with easy gradients, through trees and open country.

Start: The car park behind Holt village hall near Ham Green.

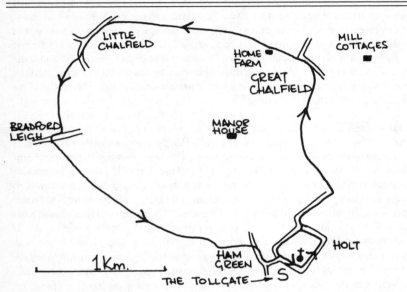

Walk back towards Ham Green (the village green) past The Old Ham Tree pub on right, bear left at the green and continue on past the parish church of St Katherine. Turn left at a footpath sign, following the church wall, then go through a kissing gate into a field. Take the next stile on the left and turn left (this is a squeezebelly stile). Continue to the main road. The wall on your left encloses **Court Gardens**. Cross over past the Holt village hall (Reading Rooms) again and along a road called The Midlands. Follow this round to the right past some large factories (Beaven's Leather Works est 1770). Notice a pump against a wall on the left referring to Holt Spa 1720. After the last factory (Sawtell's Bedding), turn left along a track. A stile takes you into a field. Go straight across and over a stile by a stream. Bear slightly to the right and at the top of the field, go over a stile and pass a coppice on your right. Cross the bridge over a stream. You should now see Great Chalfield and Mill Cottages to your left: aim for the top left corner of the field where a gate leads to a lane. Follow this on past Mill Cottages, All Saints Church and **Great Chalfield Manor**.

Continue on past a sign 'Private No Through Road' and pass Home Farm on your left. The land now opens out and leads on to Little Chalfield. Pass through an avenue of chestnut and beech trees. At the road ahead turn left and continue on past a road coming in from the right signposted South Wraxall. The road dips down and at the bottom go over a stream and turn right into a field. Follow the hedgerow on the left to the top of the field where a stile leads into a second field. Continue following the left hedgerow until you come out on to a road at Mirkens Farm. Turn right towards Bradford Leigh but turn left immediately past the first house on your left (Blackacre Cottage). Go into a field and follow the left hedgerow. The view opens out again and slightly to your right you should see the spire of Christchurch in Bradford-on-Avon. Keep straight on across the field and then, towards the right, is a gateway into the next field. Aim for the bottom left corner: the large chimney which comes into view straight ahead is the Nestle factory at Staverton. Make for the electricity pylon and then go through a gate leaving the pylon on your right and follow the hedgerow on your right. In the next field follow the hedgerow on the right round the field and then find a gap in the bottom hedgerow into the field beyond. Aim for the bottom left corner. Holt should now be visible ahead. Cross a ditch into the next field and follow the left hedgerow out to a road. Turn right and the road will lead you back to Ham Green passing The Tollgate pub.

POINTS OF INTEREST:
Court Gardens – A 7 acre National Trust garden of mystery, open (except Saturday) 2.00pm-4.30pm. 18th-century house not open to the public.
Great Chalfield Manor – Also National Trust. A 15th-century Manor House restored early this century by Major R Fuller whose family still live there. Open Tuesday-Thursday 12.00pm-1.00pm and 2.00pm-5.00pm.

REFRESHMENTS:
The Old Ham Tree (tel no: 0225 782581). Pub with garden.
The Tollgate (tel no: 0225 782326). Pub with garden.

Walk 9   A FLIGHT OF LOCKS NEAR DEVIZES $4^1/_2$m (7km)

Maps: OS Sheets Landranger 173; Pathfinder ST 86/96.

A walk along an old canal.

Start: At 977627, near the church in Rowde, north-west of Devizes.

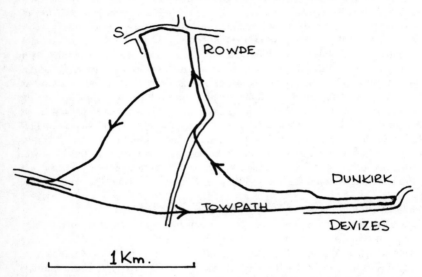

Proceed down the road away from the church and turn left at the crossroads down a path signposted **Kennet and Avon Canal**. Bear right at the fork and continue down a grassy path. Turn left over a stile and bear right down the edge of the field to a footbridge and stile by the canal. Turn left and follow the towpath for $1^1/_2$ miles to the A361 bridge. Cross the bridge and turn left and follow the road back to the canal. Pass a cottage and derelict buildings and go through a gate ahead. Cross the field diagonally, bearing right towards the house. Follow the lane to the road and turn right. After about $^1/_2$ mile turn left and return to Rowde.

POINTS OF INTEREST:

Kennet and Avon Canal – A unique flight of locks designed by John Rennie. There are 29 locks in the flight, 16 of which make a giant stairway, which enable the canal to rise 234ft. Information about the canal can be obtained at the Canal Centre on Devizes Wharf. The large ponds between the locks are the site of the annual 'Boto X' carnival event.

REFRESHMENTS:

The George Inn, Rowde (tel no: 0380 3053). Near the church. Not open until noon on weekdays.

The Black Horse (tel no: 0380 3930). Just to the right after crossing the A361 bridge.

Walk 10   **AROUND DUNDAS AQUEDUCT** $4^1/_2$m (7km)

Maps: OS Sheets Landranger 172 & 173; Pathfinder ST 86/96 & 66/76.

A walk along the Limpley Stoke valley .

Start: The lay-by on the A36 about $^1/_4$ mile north of the Viaduct Inn.

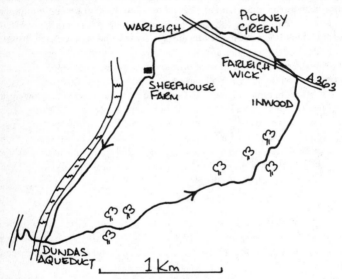

Walk down to the canal from either end of the lay-by and go left towards the bridge. Cross over and go right on the canal path which leads you over the railway (Bath to south coast) and over the River Avon. Continue along and go left of a workshop and over a stile marked 'Public Path'. Bear left and up to a stile into a field. Cross field to the top left corner and go over another stile. Turn right and follow a stone-strewn track (quite steep) to Conkwell. Bounds Cottage on the left marks the boundary between Avon/Wiltshire. Continue past cottages and turn left at the road junction. Keep on the road, passing a turning to the left, and then look for a stone stile on the left into a field at the end of a wood. Keep the wood on your left and go through the top of four fields (stiles). At the end of the fourth field go right through a gate into a field surrounded by wood. Follow the right-hand boundary, turning right at the end and down through a gate. Now go left and through another gate into a wood. Go through and over a gate into a field. Walk on with the wood on your left and pass the wall enclosing Inwood House. When you come to a gate on your left go through and up to another track by some buildings. Turn right and go out to the main road, A363, at Farleigh Wick.

Turn left and pass the Fox and Hounds (or not as the case may be). Go on for about 100 yards and take a footpath on the right, kissing gate, to Pickney Green. The path leads you diagonally across to some houses and through another kissing gate. Continue up the lane and bear left at the triangle. The cottages to the right were originally quarrymen's cottages. Cross over the next lane and down a footpath signposted Warleigh, passing Douche Farm Nursery on your left. Follow the path which turns left and, passing some cottages, go under an arch. There is now a bridleway going to the left, but you follow the narrow path straight on and down through the wood. Keep on until you come to a stile into a field. You can now see across the valley to Claverton and the American Museum building above it. Continue with a hedgerow on your right and go over a stile into a lane. Turn left and walk to Sheephouse Farm. Go straight on between the buildings until you come to two gates. Take the gate on the right and cross the small field to another gate. Now turn left and go over a stile, to a rough track which leads down towards the river. Follow on with the river on your right until you see **Dundas Aqueduct**. Go round at the back of the boathouse, over a stile and up steps to the canal path. Turn right and back to the start.

POINTS OF INTEREST:

Dundas Aqueduct – Notice the entrance to the boat base and moorings on the right. This was the start of the Somerset Coal Canal in use from 1801 to 1898 and going to Paulton with a branch to Radstock. This first part was dug out and re-opened between 1986 and 1988.

REFRESHMENTS:

The Viaduct Inn (tel no: 022122 3187).
The Fox and Hounds (tel no: 02216 3122).

Walk 11   HILPERTON AND WHADDON   4¹/₂m (7km)

Maps: OS Sheets Landranger 173; Pathfinder ST 86/96 and ST 85/95.

A walk across fields, over the Kennet and Avon Canal, and beside the River Avon.

Start: At 871592, in The Knap, near Hilperton Church.

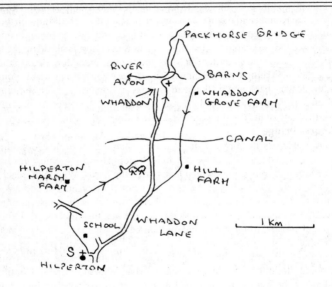

At the top of The Knap, go along the lane which leads, between houses, to the church. Here you will find a signpost, a bridleway sign pointing along the lane and a footpath sign pointing to the right. Take the footpath going off to the right. This is a short path which runs between the Old Schoolhouse, the house on the right of the lane, and a small green which has a bench seat on it. Go through a swing gate and bear slightly right, following the right-hand fence past a school, on the right, to reach a stile. Cross this and the field beyond. Go through a gateway and over a small stream, then bear right across the next field. Go over a stile and continue ahead along the path which bends right, between houses, to reach a road. Turn left, then, after 50 yards, turn right to reach the B3105. Bear right across the road, with care, to reach the track opposite, signed for

Hilperton Marsh Farm. Follow the track, but, after 20 yards, bear right through a gap and cross the field beyond towards a hedge corner. There, go ahead, with the hedge on your right. At the next corner, turn left for 20 yards, then turn right through a gap and cross a small stream. Go up the right edge of the next field, then walk ahead to reach a hedge and ditch at the far side.

Turn left for 100 yards, to where the ditch ends. Turn right, then right again for 100 yards, and, when you are opposite the corner of a copse on the left, turn left across the field and go along its top edge to reach a gate on to a lane. Turn left and follow the lane over the Kennet and Avon Canal, and on past some low buildings on the left. Now, just after the road bends left, go over a footbridge and stile on the right and cross the field beyond. Now, keeping to the right of a house, continue ahead up the left edge of two fields to reach the Church of St Mary the Virgin, Whaddon. Bear to the left of the church, then turn right to pass behind it. The River Avon is down below you on the left. Bear left down a bank and walk ahead to cross an iron bridge over Semington Brook. Bear left across the field beyond to reach a gate beside the River Avon. Turn right and follow the bank of the river, passing an old railway embankment, to reach an old stone **packhorse bridge**.

Do not cross the bridge: instead, turn sharp right, almost doubling back on yourself, and go diagonally across the field, heading towards some black barns. At the far side you will join a track which leads up to the barns. When you reach the barns, bear to their right and, after going through a gate, follow a metalled track leading up to Whaddon Grove Farm. When the track bends right, near the house, continue straight ahead, following a farm track across the field. When this track bends left into a field, go straight ahead through a gate and maintain direction to reach the Kennet and Avon Canal again. Cross the bridge over the canal and bear slightly right up the next field, aiming about 50 yards to the right of Hill Farm. At the far side, cross a stile and turn right going along the farm drive to reach a road Whaddon Lane). Continue straight ahead along the road to reach a road junction at Hilperton. Continue down Church Street for a further 200 yards, then turn right into The Knap.

POINTS OF INTEREST:
Pack Horse Bridge – The bridge is an interesting curved stone structure of unknown construction date. During the fox-hunting season, you may see a huntsman sitting on the bridge to prevent the wily old fox from using it to make its escape.

REFRESHMENTS:
The Lion and Fiddle, Hilperton.

Walk 12 SOUTH WRAXALL AND MONKTON FARLEIGH 3m (7.5km)

Maps: OS Sheets Landranger 173; Pathfinder ST 86/96.

A walk linking two old villages with views of their Manor Houses.

Start: The Longs Arms, South Wraxall.

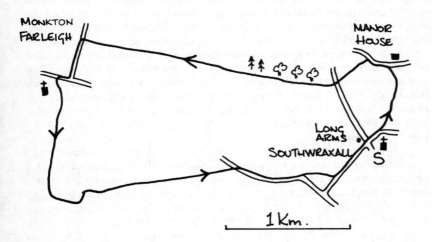

Take the road opposite the pub and go down passing St James' Church, **South Wraxall**, on your right. Follow the road round to the left and then right into Green Close. Cross between fields and over a stile just to the left of some cottages ahead. Two more stiles take you into a field where you follow the left hedgerow. The Manor House is now visible. At the end of the field go over a stile into a lane. Turn left and immediately beyond a farm on the left enter a field via two gates. Go diagonally left across the field and over two stiles into the next field. Go round a shed and out to a lane via a gate. Ahead you will see some tall iron gates and the Manor House at **Monkton Farleigh**. Go over a stile to the left of the gates and follow an avenue of trees (Norway Maples) keeping to the left of the left-hand row. Go over a stile by an iron gate, then cross and follow the right-hand hedgerow to the top and go over a stile by a cottage. Turn left in the lane and at the T-junction turn right and up to the Church of St Peter.

Straight on is The Kings Arms, should you need refreshment. The walk continues on a path immediately below the church, signposted Farleigh Wick. Cross over a stile and bear left. Go through a kissing gate and down steps to a track. Cross to a stile then go down to a stile by a gate. Continue with hedgerow on left. At the top a track comes in from the right, but you continue straight on across the next field to a stile in a wire fence. Now cross to the far left corner, and a stile goes into the next field where there is a wind pump. Do not go over the stile, but go left through a gate. Around farm buildings, left and right, you will see a gateway ahead to the next field. Go through and then left towards a wood. Follow round the edge of the wood and go over some protected barbed wire by a cattle trough. Cross to go through a gate on your right, then turn left along the track. This track leads you through three fields, passing another wind pump on the way. It then goes right, but our way is straight ahead to a gap in the hedgerow opposite. Go over a gate and straight on over the next field and down to a gate leading into a lane. Turn right and follow the lane until there is a sharp right bend. Here go over a stile immediately to the right of a telegraph pole and cross a field to a lane beyond a gateway. Turn left and follow this lane back to The Longs Arms.

POINTS OF INTEREST:
South Wraxall – St James' Church dates from the 14th or 15th century and includes the Longs Chapel. The Manor House was the home of the Long family.
Monkton Farleigh – The church of St Peter dates from the end of the 13th century and has many interesting plaques. The Manor House is the home of the Hobhouse family.

REFRESHMENTS:
The Longs Arms, South Wraxall (tel no: 02216 4450). Pub with garden.
The Kings Arms, Monkton Farleigh (tel no: 0225 858705). Pub with garden.

Walks 13 and 14 CHERHILL TO COMPTON BASSETT 5m (8km)
Maps: OS Sheets Landranger 173; Pathfinder SU 07/17.
Lanes, tracks, and farmland, with some hilly walking. Splendid views, two villages of character, and two fine churches.
Start: At 038702, the church in Cherhill village.

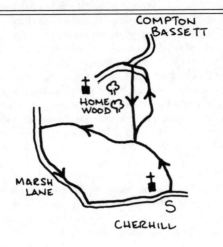

First visit the beautifully-kept church and surrounding houses in Cherhill. Leaving the churchyard turn left and walk up 'The Street'. On reaching the top, take the left-hand lane, passing Upper Farm on the right. Walk straight ahead up the metalled lane marked 'No Through Road'. This lane bends round the hillside and soon reaches a group of farm buildings, left. Pass through the blue metal gate here and immediately before the house on the right pass through another blue gate. Follow the track uphill on the left of the field. Follow the track to a small blue gate at the beginning of a wood. Pass through and follow the track past the wood, left. The track begins to descend through a sunken lane. Follow this down the hillside and keep left each time another track comes in from the right. Keep on until it joins a road opposite cottages in **Compton Bassett**.

Turn left in the village street for the church, which must be visited. Return, retracing your steps back past the track you used to reach the village. About $1/4$ mile ahead is the White Horse pub. To extend this walk, go right through the village, about $1/2$ mile, to notice the many interesting village cottages of the Compton Bassett Estate. (There is also a magnificent Manor House up the street on the left.)

Retrace your steps again back to the track where you entered the village. About 100 yards up the track there is a small stile, right, at the edge of Home Wood. Cross the stile and walk uphill with the wood on your right. Go through a small metal gate at the top and continue along the edge of the wood until you reach a wooden gate. Pass through and keep straight ahead across the field towards a house. Pass to the right of this house and gain the lane through double metal gates. Turn right here and follow this track which descends for just over $1/2$ mile down the hillside. This track ends in the road opposite an old RAF camp. Turn left and walk along the road for about 300 yards, then turn left where signposted 'Cherhill'. Follow the lane for almost $1/2$ mile and where it bends right in the village turn left into the The Street, and return to the church.

POINTS OF INTEREST:

Compton Bassett – The church, which looks quite large from outside, is surprisingly small once inside. Note the fine early 15th-century stone rood screen, and the Norman pillars in the north aisle. There is also an interesting barrel-vault, with carved bosses.

REFRESHMENTS:

The White Horse, Compton Bassett (tel no: 0249 813118).
The Black Horse, Cherhill (tel. 0249 813365). If it is preferred to take refreshment at the end of this walk, The Black Horse will be found on the main A4 road. Turn right in The Street, just before reaching the Post Office.

Walk 15   WOOTTON BASSETT TO GREENHILL   5m (8km)

Maps: OS Sheets Landranger 173; Pathfinder SU 08/18.

An easy walk, starting and finishing with some town walking.

Start: The Town Hall in High Street, Wootton Bassett.

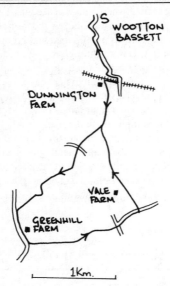

Cross the High Street, turn right and just past Touchdown House turn left down Beamans Lane. At the bottom turn right for a few yards, then left along a track past a children's playing field into Morestone Road. At the end, cross over New Road and pass through the stone bollards and down the footpath to the railway line. Turn left to the Beaufort Arms and cross the railway bridge. After the bridge, turn right down the track and after 50 yards, take a left fork towards the farm buildings. Just before the buildings enter the field on your left over a stile in the corner. Cross the field to the stile and a gap between the second and third houses opposite. Cross Dunnington Road and follow a signposted path between houses opposite to a stile into a field. Follow the hedge on the left past the light industrial estate until you reach a new footbridge over Thunderbrook. Cross the bridge (*).

Turn right and aim for a gate and a stile in the hedge opposite. Keeping in same direction make for the stile on to a road. Cross the road, bearing slightly left to a gap, with a stile and finger post, into a field. Turn half-left and cross the field diagonally to a gate by a pond and continue across the next field to the gateway or gap ahead. Keep straight ahead to another gateway about 100 yards from the bottom left-hand corner leading on to a metalled track. Cross over, turn left and go through a gate in the corner near the farm. Cross the next field where you will see glasshouses on your right, and aim for a gate half-way between the house on the left and the tree-lined pond on the right in front of more glasshouses. Turn left at the road and go uphill, and 50 yards after Upper Greenhill Farm turn left and go through a gate on the bend marked 'Public Bridleway'. Follow the downhill track into a hedge-lined lane and follow that to the gate at its end. Keep to the left of the stream to the hedge-line ahead. Fifty yards after two ponds on the left, cross over a culvert on the right but continue along the previous line of the walk to a gate in the field's right-hand corner. At this road junction do not turn left or right but continue straight along the road for 300 yards and turn left at the stile and finger post, to cross a field to a metal stile. Cross the next field in the same direction to a wire fence, narrow ditch and metal stile. Cross the next field to two hunting gates in a double hedge. Keep to the left of the pond in the next field and cross to the metal gate opposite. Cross the field to a good bridge over Thunderbrook.

Retrace your steps from the (*) on previous page to reach the **Wootton Bassett Town Hall**.

POINTS OF INTEREST:
Wootton Bassett Town Hall – Black and white on stone pillars, dated about 1690 with early 18th-century fire engine and stocks underneath. It contains a local museum open on Saturdays 10.30-12am.

REFRESHMENTS:
Emm's Restaurant, High Street, Wootton Bassett (tel no: 0793 854783). Good home-made lunches and teas.
The Town Local, Station Road (bottom), Wootton Bassett (tel no: 0793 852480). Good home cooking served midday and in the evenings.
Various local pubs in Wootton Bassett.

Walk 16   ROUNDWAY AND HEDDINGTON   5m (8km)

Maps: OS Sheets Landranger 173; Pathfinder SU 06/16 and ST 86/96.

A varied walk with one fairly steep ascent.

Start: At 014633, the telephone box in the hamlet of Roundway.

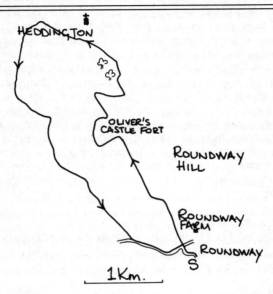

Follow the road towards Rowde for a short distance. Just after passing the private drive to Roundway Farm, look for a stile on the right. Go over this and Roundway Hill is faced. A defined path now provides the steepest part of the walk. Almost at the top of the hill a roadway is reached. Bear left along this for about $^3/_4$ mile. At a rudimentary car parking area two tracks lead off to the left. The first is the start of a nature trail providing a 1 mile circuit through attractive woodland and with long views to Salisbury Plain. This can be included in the walk if desired. The second track skirts the edge of a sharp defined bluff with the **Olivers Castle** earthwork on the right. Follow this path. On a clear day the views are extensive and impressive. The main path is shortly rejoined and, in less than $^1/_4$ mile, there is a sharp right turn. Again in less than $^1/_4$ mile look for a farm gate to the left. This is the start of a corner-cutting footpath which falls steeply

44

downhill to join the lane leading from Hill Cott to Heddington, at a stile. Should this path be missed, the roadway carries on to Hill Cott, where a sharp left turn provides the start of the lane down to Heddington. Towards the bottom of the lane, the tower of **Heddington Church** comes into view, and the lane turns sharply right. The route carries on across the front of the farm buildings, but a detour into **Heddington** for sightseeing and/or refreshments may be made by following the lane. After rejoining the route by the farm buildings, a track follows the contours around the hillside. After $^1/_2$ mile a wider trackway is crossed. Here, instead of proceeding straight across to the obvious path, look a little to the left for the start of a wide trackway along the bottom edge of a field. This is much easier to walk than the badly overgrown official path to which it runs parallel. At the next junction carry on, rising a little along a wide terraced way, with views across the Bromham area, noted for its intensive horticulture. In just under $^1/_2$ mile, as the way begins to rise, a poorly-defined path diverges to the right, making for the top edge of a small belt of woodland. Follow the hedge along the lower edge of the fields for $1^3/_4$ miles to rejoin the Rowde-Roundway road at an iron farm gate. Turn left and follow the road past the site of Roundway Mill, now a private house with the mill pond filled in, and return to Roundway hamlet.

POINTS OF INTEREST:

Olivers Castle – An ancient earthwork. At the battle of Roundway Down (1643) the victorious Royalist cavalry are believed to have pursued remnants of the defeated Parliamentary forces over the edge of Olivers Castle with considerable loss of life. Many human remains were later found buried at the foot of the bluff.

Heddington – A pleasant village with a thatched inn – The Ivy – and a village stores. The church is mainly 13th century, with an 18th-century decorated organ.

REFRESHMENTS:

The Ivy Inn, Heddington (tel no: 0380 850276).

Walk 17   LACOCK AND BOWDEN PARK $5^1/_2$m (9km)

Maps: OS Sheets Landranger 173; Pathfinder ST 86/96 & 87/97.

A walk with great panoramic views over north and west Wiltshire.

Start: The car park in Lacock.

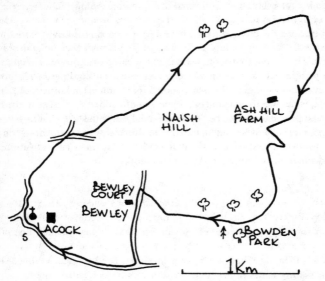

Make for the church of St Cyriac going down past the tithe barn and then right past the Carpenters Arms. Turn left opposite the church up a road signposted 'Dead End'. Two bridges take you over Bide Brook. Keep on the lane past some houses and, at the top, turn right then through a kissing gate. Go straight across the field and through a sprung gate to the road. Go on and then right to Rey bridge over the river Avon. Go over a stile on the left into a field and cross over at half-right aiming for the left-hand end of a stone wall. Go through a stile, cross the road and go through another stile. Follow this path round with a rather fierce-looking wire fence on your left, then go over a double stile into a field. Go half-left into the next field and now follow the hedgerow on the right up a slight bank. This is the towpath of the Wilts and Berks canal defunct for many a year. Continue on the left bank of the canal ditch. Go over a stile and on until you pass a collapsed brick bridge. Go over a stile to the left, cross the canal bed, which can be a bit damp, and over a gate into a field. The canal is now on your left. Follow on and through a gate into the next field, cross this and go over a gate (with some barbed wire). Cross another dampish patch and go over a broken stile into a field. Climb up the bank and then cross towards the right-hand edge of the hedgerow opposite. Carry on with the hedgerow now on your left, then go through a gate and across another field and over a gate to a track. Follow this until you come to a farm road, where you turn right for a long climb up Naish Hill.

Continue on the road through a wood and on past Ash Hill Farm on your right. Follow the road until you come to a T-junction where you turn left and up past Naish Hill Quarry. Just before the first house on the right go through a gate and cross the field to a stile. Cross a narrow paddock and go over another stile. Cross the field diagonally to the left and go over a stile into a wood. Follow on, but go right when you come to a path junction. At a stile go over and out of the wood. Follow on with a wood on your right. The path leads down to the right and you will see Bowden Park on your left, a fine house with large bow windows built in the late 18th century. Go down and through a gate in the next field, and cross to the bottom right. Go over a gate and follow the hedgerow on the right. Go over a stile, through some bushes and out to the road. Turn left and follow the road past Bewley Grange and on to a T-junction where the Bell is to your left, but turn right and follow the road back to **Lacock.**

POINTS OF INTEREST:
Lacock – A National Trust village with Lacock Abbey and many beautiful cottages.

REFRESHMENTS:
Several pubs and tea places in Lacock.
The Bell, Bewley (tel no: 024973 308). A nice pub with a large garden.

Walk 18 SOMERFORD COMMON AND BRAYDON WOOD $5^1/_2$m (9km)

Maps: OS Sheets Landranger 173; Pathfinder SU 08/18.

A walk leading through the pleasant farmland of north Wiltshire.

Start: At 024863, the edge of Somerford Common. Park beside the road.

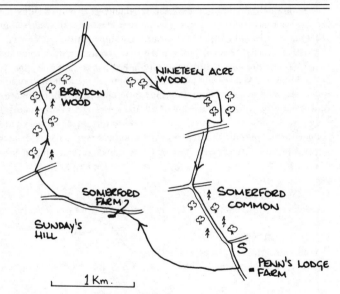

In a couple of places the footpaths have not been well maintained, so be prepared for a certain amount of trail blazing! Walk back down the road away from the common towards Penn's Lodge Farm. Opposite the farm entrance turn right on to the broad track and follow it for 1 mile or so, always keeping the hedge on your left. Look out for pleasant views on your left particularly of Brinkworth church. After a while the path leads through a copse and then broadens out into a grassy track between hedges. At the gate near Somerford Farm follow the track to the right of the gate ahead and turn left on to the road. Proceed along the road, passing Sundays Hill Farm and, after the road bends to the left, go through the next gate in the right-hand hedge. Immediately go through the wooden gate on the left and, bearing right, cross the field, keeping to the

48

left of the oak tree in the middle. Negotiate the rickety stile in the opposite hedge and go through the gate on the other side of the road. Follow the broad track (a Right of Way) through Braydon Wood, until you come out on to another road. Turn right, passing the water tower, and proceed to the houses just before a T-junction. A long track leads away to the right from these buildings to a distant farm. Keep, as far as is possible, close to the hedge to the right of this track.

When you reach the field in front of the wood, bear left to the corner of the wood. Climb the rickety gate and take the left-hand track which hugs the inside edge of Nineteen Acre Wood. The bridleway leaves the wood at the point where the path bends right for the second time, so continue straight on here. A scramble through the undergrowth will bring you out on to a broad, grassy area. Continue straight on towards the wood keeping the hedge on your left. The gate into the wood is too overgrown to negotiate, but it is an easy matter to skirt round it along a small path which leads into the undergrowth. Go straight on at the crossroads, then turn right through the first gate and follow the path to the bottom of the hill. Turn right here, then left after the stile, and continue to the road. Follow the track on the other side of the road leading through Somerford Common. When you reach another road, cross over again and keep on. Eventually you will emerge from the common close to your starting point.

Walk 19   **BIDDESTONE AND SLAUGHTERFORD** $5^1/_2$m (9km)
Maps: OS Sheets Landranger 173; Pathfinder ST 87/97.
A walk starting in open country and the By Brook valley.
Start: By the pond in Biddestone village.

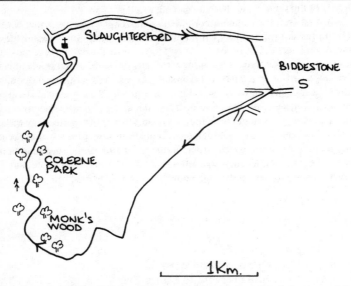

Walk away from the White Horse pub and, with the pond on your left, go straight on
along Hartham Lane with the **Church of St Nicholas** on your right. Bear left here.
When the road takes a left turn bear right by the cemetery and follow road marked to
Field Barn Farm only. When the road turns right, go straight on to a footpath marked
'Weavern'. There are now open views all round: the church tower slightly to the right
on the horizon is Colerne. The footpath goes straight on, then over an iron stile. The
path beyond heads towards a large single tree. Follow a hedgerow on your left which
leads down to a gate and a lane. Go right here and down the lane until you come to a
gate on the left down between a wire fence and a hedgerow. Go through two more gates
past a copse, then over a stile by a stream. Bear right (not over stream), then cross a
footbridge over the main By Brook stream near a small weir. Go over the stile into
Monk's Wood, and then take a path to the right leading up to a stile.

You have an option here: go over the stile and up the field to a lane, go straight on, then take a track on the right going back towards the wood; or keep following the woodland path, bearing left when the path divides and coming out at the Keeper's Cottage, where the alternative routes will rejoin. Go straight on down the main track through the wood of Colerne Park. Go over a gate and continue through an avenue of oak and pine trees. Go through a gate and out to a lane. Turn right and walk down into Slaughterford passing a paper mill originally built about 150 years ago. Continue over the By Brook and follow the road round to the left through the village, passing **St Nicholas Church**.

Keep on the road, passing a turning to the left and start to climb up out of the valley. After $^1/_2$ mile or so the road bends to the left and there is a footpath sign on the right. Go over a gate and follow the stone wall on the left. Now go right along the field boundary and over a stile. Keep on this direction across the next field towards a stile visible in the hedgerow ahead. After going over this stile the footpath goes diagonally to the right and out to a lane over the brow of the hill. Alternatively you can go round the left-hand border of the field and over a stile, cross another field and over a stile then out to the lane by a large stone slab stile.

Turn left to Biddestone village pond.

POINTS OF INTEREST:

Church of St Nicholas, Biddestone – Dating back to the 14th century and with all boxed pews. The gallery was put up and used by Slaughterford parishioners after Cromwell destroyed their church.

Church of St Nicholas, Slaughterford – A small church in the middle of a field. The church was re-built and re-opened in 1823 after lying in ruins for 200 years. The tower dates from the 13th century and is original.

REFRESHMENTS:

The White Horse, Biddestone (tel no: 0249 713305). Pub with garden.

Walk 20   **CASTLE COMBE AND LONG DEAN**   5¹/₂m (9km)
Maps: OS Sheets Landranger 173; Pathfinder ST 87/97.
A walk on good paths and lanes.
Start: The signposted free car park, Castle Combe.

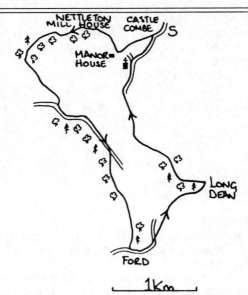

Walk downhill then right at a T-junction. At a bend in the road go ahead on a path signposted Nettleton Shrub and pass the school on the right. The path bears to the right. Go over a stile by a gate, not along the tarmac path to the right. Once over the stile go left and follow a fence at first, then a stone wall. Another stile leads to a wall which is kept on your left. Do not go over the next stile, but follow the path to the right with first a wall then a fence on your left. The path leads to a stone bridge over a stream and then opens to a track. To your left is the Manor House, now an hotel. Continue on the track and over two stiles. The track now goes right and through a tall, stone-surrounded kissing gate. This was Nettleton Mill House, now much modernised!

   The path goes to the left between two houses. Go over a stile and on with the stream to your left. Beware of a six-foot muddy patch caused by a spring, and continue to a stone slab bridge. Turn left over this and go up a track, which is steep at first, to reach a lane. Turn left and follow the lane to a road. Turn left again, following the road to a road junction. If you are tired a left turn will take you into Castle Combe village, but our route goes through a gate on the right and takes the footpath left signposted 'Ford 1 mile'. Go over a stile and along a path keeping to the top of the valley until you come to a post which indicates a footpath along and down. Now go down towards the trees, then over a large stone stile and over a wooden bridge. Follow the path across a field and through trees to reach a wire fence. Continue along the path to reach a stile. Go over and follow the lane beyond to Ford and the main road. Across the road and down another lane is the White Hart for food and drink.

Our route goes left at the main road and after about 40 yards left again. Shortly, a stile on the right with a signpost for 'Long Dean' is taken to a path diagonally across the field and through trees. Go through a gate and between banks towards Long Dean. There used to be two woollen mills here, both now converted to houses. Go on, bearing left past the post box and Rose Cottage. The track leads towards the sewage works, but at the gate bear right and continue over a stone stile by a gate. The path gradually descends towards By Brook. There is another stile to cross and a gate to go through before a stone bridge takes you over By Brook to the road. Turn right into **Castle Combe**. After a look round this most attractive village and a visit to the White Hart go back up the hill to the car park.

POINTS OF INTEREST:
Castle Combe – Cannot fail to interest with its Market Cross, the church of St Andrew, a well-tended memorial and a general peace and tranquillity. Part of the film Dr Dolittle was made here.

REFRESHMENTS:
The White Hart Inn, Ford. Pub with garden.
The White Hart Inn, Castle Combe. Pub with family room.

Walk 21   BISHOPS CANNINGS AND WANSDYKE   6m (9.5km)

Maps: OS Sheets Landranger 173; Pathfinder SU 06/16.

A walk combining downland with the towpath of the Kennet and Avon canal.

Start: At 037644, the car park in Bishops Cannings.

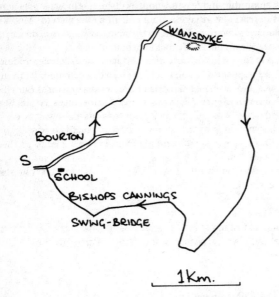

Take the metalled road signposted 'Bourton, Easton, No Through Road'. Bear left at the village school (Bourton Road) and follow the lane to Bourton hamlet. At Bourton take the left fork signposted 'No Through Road'. Fork right shortly and climb steadily until meeting the ridge of Wansdyke near the top of the hill. Behind, there are ever expanding views of the Pewsey Vale, across to Salisbury Plain. Turn right over a stile and follow the Wansdyke (see Walk 32) earthwork towards Tan Hill.

To the left the Cherhill Monument is visible about $2\frac{1}{2}$ miles away. At the third stile turn right on to a track along the edge of a field, heading for a water tower on the horizon. At the water tower go through the gate and continue down a lane, passing strip lynchets and farm buildings until the Devizes-Pewsey road is reached. Turn right, cross the Kennet and Avon canal and descend to the towpath. Follow the towpath towards

Devizes. On reaching an interesting swing bridge, cross the canal and bear left to return to **Bishops Cannings**. The reason why the village church is known as the 'Little Steeple' will now be evident!

POINTS OF INTEREST:
Bishops Cannings – A charming village with one of Wiltshire's finest parish churches, almost entirely Early English. The village is the home of the Wiltshire 'Moonraker' legend. In the 19th century villagers were caught by a customs and excise man while raking the pond in the dead of night. They quickly explained they were trying to bring in the large cheese, clearly seen floating out on the surface. The 'zizeman' rode away, laughing at their stupidity – the 'cheese' was only the reflection of the full moon! But the villagers had the last laugh – they had in fact been caught starting to take in a hidden cache of smuggled brandy! Hence the nickname for Wiltshire folk – 'Moonrakers'.

REFRESHMENTS:
The Crown, Bishops Cannings (tel no: 038086 218).

Walk 22 WOOTTON BASSETT TO BUSHEY VOWLEY 6m (9.5km)
Maps: OS Sheets Landranger 173; Pathfinder SU 08/18.
An easy walk, starting and finishing with town walking.
Start: The Town Hall, High Street, Wootton Bassett.

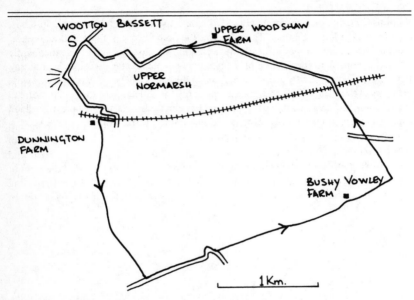

Walk down the High Street in the direction of Lyneham, and at the crossroads at the bottom turn left and go down New Road until you see stone bollards opposite Morstone Road. Turn right here and go along a path to the railway line. Turn left to the Beaufort Arms and cross the railway bridge. After the bridge turn right down the track and after 50 yards take a left fork towards farm buildings. Just before tin buildings enter a field on the left by means of a stile in the corner. Cross the field to another stile and a gap between the second and third houses opposite. Cross Dunnington Road and follow the signposted path between the houses opposite to a stile into a field. Follow the hedge on the left past the light industrial estate until you reach a new footbridge over Thunderbrook. Cross over the bridge and straight across the field, keeping the hedge on your left. Go through the metal gate about 50 yards from the left-hand corner of the field. Cross the next field to pass the side of a pond in the corner to two hunting gates set in a double hedge. Cross over the next field and make for the metal stile, narrow ditch and wire, then go over the next field keeping close to the right-hand hedge. Go over another metal stile and then walk ahead to a wooden stile, by a finger post, which brings you on to a road.

Turn left and go along the road for about $^1/_2$ mile to a junction. Turn right for about 200 yards. On the left just before farm buildings you will see a metal gate and a finger post marked 'Public Bridleway'. Go through the gate and cross the next four fields keeping close to the hedge on your right. Continue until you see Bushy Vowley Farm. Skirt round the property through the gate on your left to reach the metalled track across the field between wire fences. This is the Public Bridleway. Walk to its end to Bincknoll Lane. The lane has wide grass verges on either side. Turn left and continue over the old canal and the railway bridge. Beyond the railway take the left fork and continue to a roundabout. Turn left, passing Woodshaw Inn on your right, and continue up the hill to the roundabout using the footpath behind the hedge on the right. At the roundabout turn left into Noremarsh Road then cross over at Washbourne Road on your right, and go up to the top. At the end turn left and enter Old Court Playing Field to the right of Noremarsh School gate. Cross the playing field and turn left along Old Court, passing the old Church School, now the Community Centre, on your left. Turn right and return to the Town Hall (see Walk 15).

REFRESHMENTS:
The Woodshaw Inn, Wootton Bassett, (tel no: 0793 854617). Good pub food.
Emm's Restaurant, High Street, Wootton Bassett (tel no: 0793 854783). Good home-made lunches and teas.
The Town Local, Station Road, Wootton Bassett (tel no: 0793 852480). Good home cooking served midday and in the evenings.
Various other pubs in Wootton Bassett.

Walk 23 AROUND WOOTTON BASSETT LAKE 6m (9km)

Maps: OS Sheets Landranger 173; Pathfinder SU 08/18.

A mainly flat walk with some hills. Excellent views.

Start: At 072839, the car park at Wootton Bassett Lake.

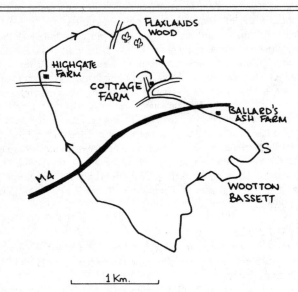

Go down the path to the left, cross the bridge and go right round the lake and up a track on the right. Go over another bridge and up to the right past a concrete culvert. At the houses turn right along a track towards Red Lodge. Here there are fine views to the Bristol Channel. Turn right before a house gate and go along a track a few yards to a gateway. Go through, turn sharp left and down the slope. At the bottom turn left and follow the left-hand hedges at the top of the slope. Pass through a gap in the hedge between fields and head for the church to reach a hedge. Turn right and go down the field still with the hedge on your left. Go through a gap into the next field and proceed in the same direction. Cross the brook, turn left and follow the left-hand hedge to trees. Turn right to join a track and follow the hedge on the left for 30 yards to a gap.

Turn left and follow the brook to where another footpath crosses near willow trees. Turn right up the track towards a clump of beech trees and a stile. Cross over and follow the path passing red-brick cottages on your left. Make for the stile opposite.Turn right and go diagonally to a brook. Cross and follow the left-hand hedge for 30 yards. Climb over the left-hand fence and follow the brook on the left. Turn right at the end and follow the hedge to a gate. Go through and on to a farm track.Turn right and walk under the motorway bridge. Go through the gate and follow the track past a second hedge before a farmhouse. Turn immediately left and cross a stile in the corner to go towards Withy Bed Wood with Park Grounds Farm on your right. Walk along the outside of the wood (on your left) to a gate. Continue across the next field to a metal gate. Cross the next field to a gateway to the left of Highgate Farm. There are good views behind you to Lyneham Bank on the right, the Ridgeway on the left and Cherhill Monument straight in front.

Cross the road and pass the farm on your right. If the footpath in front is blocked follow the track round the farm buildings to a gate on the left. Cross the field to a gate half-way along the opposite hedge. Follow the hedge on your left to a fence half-way and rejoin the public footpath. Turn right and walk past Seven Island Pond keeping woods about 200 yards to your left. Make for a gap in the hedge opposite and cross to Purley Farm. Go between farm buildings and take the farm track to the road at Oaklands Farm Industrial Estate. Turn left at the road and after 100 yards go right through a gate to enter a field with an electricity pylon. Make for the right-hand corner and go through a gate, under the wires, into Flaxlands Wood. Walk along the track to a gate but do not go through. Instead, turn right and then left at a small track and continue to the end of the wood keeping as close as possible to the edge. Go through into a field and follow the left-hand hedge to a narrow gate. Cross the next field in the same line in the direction of Midgehall Copse. Get under an over fence and cross what may be a boggy patch to the road. Turn right and walk to Cottage Farm, then turn left to the B4042 road. Turn left and walk along the verge under the motorway bridge. Continue to Ballard's Ash Farm and The Knoll and back to the starting point.

REFRESHMENTS:
The Prince of Wales at Coped Hall Roundabout 200 yards from the lake car park (tel no: 0793 852388). Children welcome. Good play facilities.

Maps: OS Sheets Landranger 173; Pathfinder SU 08/18.
A mostly flat walk over fields and through woods.
Start: At 025860, Penn's Lodge Farm, Stoppers Hill Road, Brinkworth.

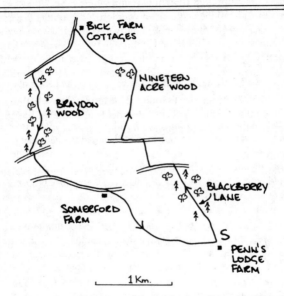

From Penn's Lodge Farm walk up the lane to Milbourne Common Wood and enter at a Forestry Commission sign. The path could be wet in the hollow for the first few yards. Climb up through the woods following the track for 1 mile until you reach the lane at the end. Enter the lane and turn left. Walk along this quiet lane for the length of two fields on your right. Go through a gate and follow the left-hand hedge to a gate opposite on to a road. Turn left on the road, walk along to the track on your right leading to Worthy Hill Farm and pass between house and buildings to the right-hand corner of Nineteen Acre Wood. Enter the wood and walk straight ahead along the wide path to the crossed paths. Keep straight on and follow the inside edge of the wood across its northern end. Go to the end of the track. Here go through a gate on your right. Make for the gateway opposite at the right-hand side of a short hedge and cross diagonally to the gate. Do not go through, but walk in the direction of Bick Farm Cottages keeping the hedge on your left. Go into the road, turn left and walk along it with the water tower on your right. Continue around the bend and go downhill to look at the pond at Braydon. Return a few yards and look for a gateway on your right. Do not be put off by the 'Strictly Private' sign: this is a public Right of Way and only the side paths are private. Follow the good track through **Braydon Wood** which is very pretty.

Pass the keeper's wooden cottage on your left and continue to a gate on to a lane. Cross over the lane and go over the stile slightly to your left. Cross the field to the left-hand corner with a farm on your right. Go through two gates on to a lane, turn left and walk past Sundayshill House and Tanglin Farm gateway to Somerford Farm. At the bend in the road go through the gateway ahead and walk along the bridleway between two hedges. At the end of the path go through a gate and cross the field, keeping the hedge on your right. The edge curves round to the left and you will find a pylon straight in front of you on the skyline. Cross the next fields in a straight line to Penn's Lodge Farm in Stoppers Hill Road and return to the start.

POINTS OF INTEREST:

Braydon Wood – Once part of the forest that stretched from the Thames Valley to Dorset. Its first mention is in a charter of 796 and Saxon Kings hunted here.

REFRESHMENTS:

The Three Crowns, Brinkworth (tel no: 066 641 366) on the B4042. The young landlord has won the nationwide Guinness Award for the best one course pub meal, so the food is good.

Walk 25 WOOTTON BASSETT AND LYDIARD TREGOZE 6m (9.5km)

Maps: OS Sheets Landranger 173; Pathfinder SU 08/18.

A walk across farmland to Lydiard Country Park.

Start: The public car park, High Street, Wootton Bassett.

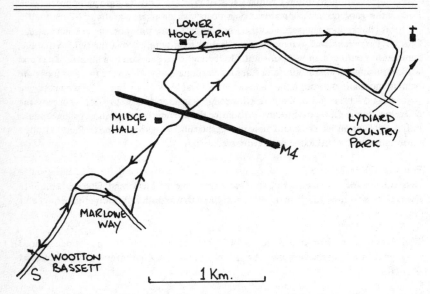

Leaving the car park turn right into High Street and walk for about $^1/_2$ mile until a Mobil garage is reached on the other side of the road. Just past the garage turn right into Marlowe Way and continue until reaching Tennyson Road on the right. Just past this turn left on to a short footpath in front of a bungalow on the left side of the road. A few yards bring you to the main A3102 road. Cross over towards a bungalow, left. Enter the farm gate here and cross directly ahead over the field. On reaching the top of this slight rise Midge Hall Farm will be seen ahead. Steer across the fields to pass the farm on your left. As the M4 motorway is approached bear right to cross the bridge over it. On the other side continue straight ahead for $^1/_2$ mile across the fields, emerging in the lane at Lower Hook Farm. Turn right in the lane, passing the farm, and immediately after this lane bends to the right, passing a cottage, left. There is a series of fence stiles into the farmland on the left. Cross these four stiles and continue forward towards the woods ahead. Walking across this last field bear half-left towards the barbed wire fence which bounds the field. Keep this fence on your left as the field narrows to a kissing gate and stile. Cross and head for the waymarked stile a few yards ahead. Cross this and walk straight ahead towards the gap in the trees which soon becomes a glade in the woods surrounding **Lydiard Country Park.**

Enter the glade and walk ahead. Signposts will soon be seen to the Mansion, the Visitors' Centre, the Church, and the Pheasantry. After possible refreshment at the Visitors' Centre, walk down the road to the park exit, which runs from the front of the Centre. On gaining the road turn right and follow the lane for about $^1/_2$ mile to reach Lower Hook Farm again. (If preferred, the return may be made over the farmland walk used to approach the Park.)

Pass Lower Hook Farm and continue along the lane, passing Hook Farm, next on the right, and then a small cemetery. Just after this there is a stile, left, which leads into a field. Walk straight across this field and in the following field bear half-left to return to the path which leads to the motorway bridge. After crossing the motorway, and then passing Midge Hall Farm again, a route should be taken slightly right aiming for the garage buildings across the field. At the Esso garage cross the main road and use the footpath between a bungalow, right, and the Timbervale Guest House, left. This emerges very shortly in Marlowe Way and thence to Wootton Bassett High Street and the start of the walk.

POINTS OF INTEREST:

Lydiard Country Park – From Tudor times Lydiard Park was the seat of a prominent local family, the St Johns. The house was remodelled in 1743. A number of the ground-floor rooms are open to the public, on weekdays and Saturdays from 10.00am-1.00pm and from 2.00pm-5.30pm, on Sundays 2.00pm-5.30pm. Admission free. The church, behind the house, must be visited for its wonderful array of monuments including the magnificent gilded figure of Edward St John, a Royalist member of the family, who was killed at the Battle of Newbury in 1645; the wildlife in the marshy ground below the house should also be visited.

REFRESHMENTS:

There are many in the High Street, Wootton Bassett.

The Borough Arms (tel no: 0793 854833).

The Angel Hotel (tel no: 0793 852314).

The Cross Keys Inn (tel no: 0793 852326).

There is also a small refreshments facility at Lydiard Country Park.

Walk 26   BRADFORD-ON-AVON AND IFORD   6½m (10.5km)

Maps: OS Sheets Landranger 172 & 173; Pathfinder ST 65/75, 66/76, 85/95 and 86/96.

A walk by woods, fields, the rivers Avon and Frome, and the Kennet and Avon Canal.

Start: The car park by railway station in Bradford-on-Avon.

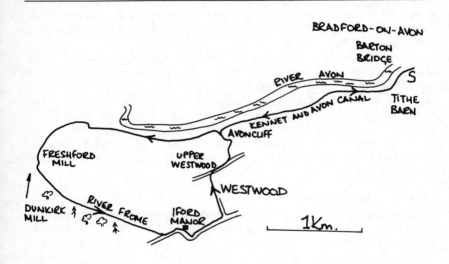

This walk can be shortened to 4 miles by starting at Avoncliff, but parking is limited. Walk to the end of the car park away from the station and take a path which passes under the railway. With the river Avon on your right, cross a grassed area to a broad path by Barton Bridge and continue on, passing the Tithe Barn on your left. The path continues on and up a slope to the Kennet and Avon Canal. Follow the towpath with the canal left and the river below right until you come to Avoncliff where the canal turns right and crosses the river and railway. Do not cross, but take a path to the right towards The Cross Guns. Turn back to go under the canal and continue on past a house offering teas. Passing The Old Court, once weavers' homes, the path leads on between hedgerows. With the river below on your right go over a stile and cross a field following the river.

Go over a stile into a wood. A path takes you through the wood and out into a field by a kissing gate. As you cross this field you come to the river Frome and if you look back you can see where it joins the Avon which goes away under the railway bridge.

The path brings you through a kissing gate at Freshford Bridge. Cross over and enter a field on the left by another kissing gate. Follow the path and shortly go right up into the wood and then through a kissing gate. Bear left and follow the path down. This up and down is quite steep. The down brings you to the river Frome, left, and over a stile. With a wire fence on your right follow on over a stile and out to the road at Freshford Mill. Go up the road, not over the river, and take the bridle path on the left by Dunkirk Mill Cottage. This leads to Dunkirk Mill (dating from the 18th century but now flats). The path then goes on between wire fences and through a gate. Bear left, down and over a small stream. Go left about 20 yards, then right. The area here is called Friary and once housed lay brothers from Hinton Priory. Go over a stile into the field and cross it keeping to the left. Go over a stile into a wood, continue on but bear left at path junction, and over a stile into a field with the river on your left. Cross the length of this field and over a stile into a lane at **Iford**.

Turn left and go down over a bridge where Britannia is on guard. Turn right at Iford Manor and follow up the steep road to Iford gatehouse and the main road. Turn right and go along until you see a road, The Pastures, on the left through a housing estate. Follow this road and at the end bear left between numbers 45 and 47 to a path and stile into Upper Westwood. Go right and continue until you see a signpost on the right but pointing left for Avoncliff. Turn left here and go down past Westwood Stone Mine until you see a path signed 'Avoncliff and Winsley'. Follow this path through a half-barrier down to Avoncliff when you retrace the canal path back to Bradford-on-Avon (see Walk 7), and the starting point.

POINTS OF INTEREST:
Iford – Iford Manor appears in Domesday Book. In 1899 it was acquired by Harold Peto who created a tiered garden in Italian style. It is open under the National Gardens scheme on Wednesday and Sunday afternoons 2-5 in July and August. Iford Bridge is thought to have been built by monks from Hinton Charterhouse about 1400. The figure of Britannia was erected by Harold Peto.

REFRESHMENTS:
The Cross Guns, Avoncliff (tel no: 02216 2335). Pub with garden.
The Inn, Freshford (tel no: 022122 2250). Pub with garden.
A selection in Bradford-on-Avon.

Walk 27   DAUNTSEY AND GREAT SOMERFORD   8m (13km)

Maps: OS Sheets Landranger 173; Pathfinder ST 88/98.
A varied, attractive walk along good tracks.
Start: At 983822, Ridgeway Lane, Dauntsey.

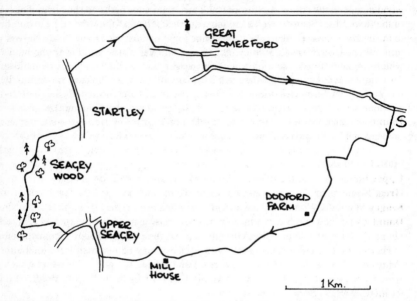

Walk down the metalled track of Ridgeway Lane to the Works. Turn right and walk in front of galvanised iron buildings and then continue along the track across the field to a metal barn on your right. Turn left and continue along a good track until you reach Dodford Farm. Enter the farmyard and turn right between buildings to continue on the track straight ahead which follows the river Avon. The track peters out at a bridge over a brook. Cross the bridge and continue across the field to the attractive weir. Cross the weir to Mill House. Turn right and continue up the track between houses for 200 yards to the finger post pointing to Upper Seagry. Turn left here and cross the field to a gate half-way along the opposite hedge. Keep straight across the field keeping to the left of a wire fence and go through a gate. Follow the track to your right between a hedge and the wire until you reach the finger post at the road pointing to **Upper Seagry**. Cross the road and the field opposite and go through the farmyard of Manor Farm on to the road.

66

Turn right into the village with its attractive stone houses and continue until you reach a crossroads with the New Inn, a free house, on your left.

Turn left at the pub and go down the hill past the houses looking for a finger post on the right pointing to Lower Stanton. Cross over the stile and follow the hedge to a wooden gate in the corner. Go through and turn right and follow the hedge to the end of the field. Enter **Seagry Wood** and where a track crosses, turn right and walk north to the end of the woods. Turn right and make for Clove Farm on the road. At the road turn left and walk through Startley. At Grove Farm turn right. Walk up a good track which becomes more of a bridleway until you reach a metalled track across the end. Turn right and continue down the track until you join the road. Follow the road to the left into **Great Somerford** until you reach the school. At the school turn left and continue to the crossroads. Continue straight on along the road until you reach **Dauntsey** Church Bridge after about $1^1/_4$ mile. Pass Dauntsey House on your left and proceed until you reach Ridgeway Lane.

POINTS OF INTEREST:

Upper Seagry – An attractive Cotswold stone village.

Great Somerford – Another attractive Cotswold stone village.

Seagry Woods – With luck, badgers may be seen here.

Dauntsey – The church contains an extremely rare 15th-16th century 30ft painted Doom Board showing the delights of Heaven and the horrors of Hell. It really needs to be seen in daylight. If the church is closed keys may be obtained from the house opposite.

REFRESHMENTS:

The New Inn, Upper Seagry (tel no: 0249 721083), a free house serving home-cooked food.

Walk 28   **BRADENSTOKE AND GREAT WOOD**   6³/₄m (11km)

Maps: OS Sheets Landranger 173; Pathfinder SU 07/17 and SU 08/18.

Hilly, wooded country with views towards the Bristol Channel.
Start: At 001794, St Mary the Virgin Church, Bradenstoke.

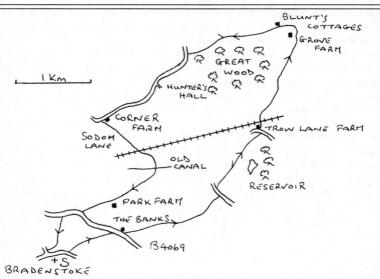

Facing the church, turn left along the road through the village. Shortly after a right bend, with St Mary's Close on the right, turn left up a short side road. Bear left across Boundary Close to reach a path, just to the left of a brick wall. Follow a track between houses and, when this ends, continue along a path between fences, with good views to the left. Continue past bungalows on the right to reach a road (the B4069). Cross, with care, and turn right for 20 yards. Now, just past a house (7 The Banks), turn left, up steps, and go along an enclosed path to reach a bungalow, on the right. Go ahead, through a gate, and along the left edge of a field. At the far corner, turn right for 20 yards, then turn left through a gap. Turn left and, just before the field corner, turn right. Now, do not go through the gate in the corner: instead, go along the field edge for 30 yards, then turn left through a gap in the hedge and go diagonally right across the field beyond. Go over a stile and along the right-hand edge of the next field to reach a minor road.

68

Bear left across the road and go over the stile opposite. Head across the middle of the field and cross two stiles at the far side. Maintain direction across the next field: there is a pond (reservoir) down to your right. Go through a gate and bear slightly right across three fields, with stiles between, to reach a lane. Turn left. Go past the first footpath sign on your right and, after a further 20 yards, turn right through some farm gates. Go to the right of the farmhouse and immediately turn left along a track, crossing the railway. Bear right up a narrow field and cross a farm track to reach a gap/gate in the top hedge. Go up the right edge of the field and cross a corner stile into the upper right-hand field. Go up the left edge of this field and, at the top corner, turn right, keeping the hedge on your left. At the hedge corner, turn left, still with the hedge/fence on the left. At the next corner, go down through a hedge gap into a wild meadow. Great Wood is now on your left. Keep to the left edge for 25 yards, then go left over a stile. Bear right down the field, heading to the right of Grove Farm. At the bottom, do NOT turn left into the farm yard: instead, go through the gate into the next field and turn left along its edge, with the buildings on your left. At a hedge corner, bear slightly right across the field to reach a stile and farm track. Cross the track and go along another track, just opposite. Pass Blunt's Cottages, on the right, and continue across the middle of a long, narrow field. Great Wood is over to your left. Maintain direction across the next field to reach a corner of the wood. Now ignore paths going right, turning left along the wood edge. Cross a stile and footbridge and bear left across the next field to reach a gate in the far left corner. Go through and turn left along a road, following it for about a mile, passing a road, going left, at Hunger's Hall. Where the road turns sharp right, at Corner Farm, turn left along Sodom Lane. Follow the lane under the railway, then over a disused canal. Just after passing a house on the left, turn right over a footbridge and stile in the hedge. Bear left across a field and go through the gate at the far side. Bear right across the next two fields and go through a gate to the right of Park Farm to join a farm track. Turn right and follow the track to reach the B4069. Cross, and turn right. After 300 yards, turn left through a gate and walk up a field to go through a second gate. Bear diagonally right across the field beyond to go through a third gate. Bear left and pass to the right of a small enclosed pond, heading towards the houses of Bradenstoke. Just before the houses, turn right over a stile and cross a paddock to reach a road. Turn left to reach a road junction. Turn right to return to the church. The ruins of Bradenstoke Abbey, which once rivalled Malmesbury, are $\frac{1}{4}$ mile along the road, past the Cross Keys Inn.

REFRESHMENTS:
The Cross Keys, Bradenstoke.
The Peterborough Arms, Dauntsey Lock.

Walk 29   AROUND BISHOPS CANNINGS   8m (13km)

Maps: OS Sheets Landranger 173; Pathfinder SU 06/16.
A downland walk starting along Wansdyke.
Start: At 020672, the car park at Smallgrain Plantation.

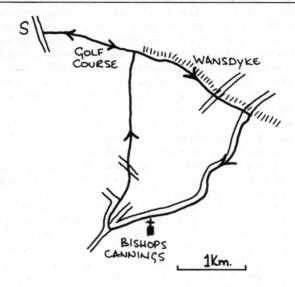

From the far end of the picnic site go through the exit behind a bungalow, left. This leads to a sunken path – the Wansdyke Ditch (see Walk 21) which goes up the hill to the Wansdyke Nature Reserve. Half-way up the hill there is a sign 'The Roman Road'. Ignore the large gate and track here and bear right through the smaller gate on to a bridleway. Continue ahead and go over the stile. At the top a track crosses the Wansdyke path with a beech clump, Furze Knoll, right. Keep straight ahead as the path descends the downs to the A361 about 1 mile ahead. Cross the main road and pass left of a farm building. Walk up the Wansdyke which climbs the down ahead. Soon a stile is reached. Cross this and turn right into a chalk lane. (There is another fine stretch of the Wansdyke on the left.) Descend on this farm track for just over 1 mile (fine views) until it emerges on the village lane at Bourton. Bear right here and follow the lane forward for about ¹/₂ mile until a crossroads (see Walk 21) is reached. Turn left here and

70

the fine church of Bishops Cannings may be visited on the left. The next building left is the Crown Inn (very good pub grub).

Retrace your steps from church or inn to the crossroads. Now turn left, marked 'West End' and follow the village street for about $^1/_2$ mile until the dual carriageway section of the A361 is reached. Cross this busy road carefully and immediately opposite there is a farm lay-by with several gates. Bear right here and follow the track up the hillside for about 300 yards to a copse. Just after the track bends sharply left there is a gate on the right into the copse. Pass through and follow the path through the copse. On emerging into a field at the far side, walk along the track on the left edge. Shortly this track reaches a road which cross and pass through the farmyard opposite. Follow the track as it curves up the hill towards Furze Knoll which can be seen again ahead. Turn left into the Wansdyke Ditch at the top to reach the car park.

REFRESHMENTS:
The Crown Inn, Bishops Cannings (tel no: 038086 218).
The Jolly Miller, Quemerford (tel no: 0249 812272).
(The Jolly Miller is left towards Calne about $^1/_2$ mile from the junction of the unclassified road to Smallgrain and the A4 to Calne. Recommended for food.)

Walk 30   **DEVIZES, SEEND AND POULSHOT**   8¹/₂m (13.5km)
Maps: OS Sheets Landranger 173; Pathfinder Sheet ST 85/95.
This walk includes the most spectacular section of the Kennet and Avon canal.
Start: At the Wharf car park behind Devizes police station.

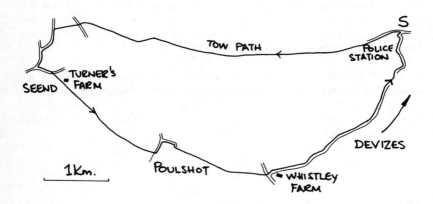

On leaving the car park cross the canal (see Walk 9) by the obvious road bridge to reach the towpath. Proceed in a westerly direction to soon reach the top lock and main road. The canal is crossed at the Nursery. Carry on, admiring the long views over the Avon Valley, as the canal descends steeply. At the last lock cross to the right-hand side of the canal, just before reaching old railway abutments. Go under a main road bridge and leave the canal by the next road, heading south towards **Seend**.

On reaching the main Trowbridge to Devizes road turn left to reach Inmarsh Lane (signposted to Worton and Bulkington). Proceed through Turner's farmyard. Look out for a finger post sign to Poulshot, go over a stile and make for another stile at the far end of the field. The path continues downhill in a straight line, through two gates, to reach a small bridge in the right-hand corner of the next field. After crossing

Summerham Brook, keep to the right and climb to a stile. Follow the bridleway, turning left then right just before reaching Poulshot, close to the Raven Inn. Cross the road and follow a broad track which runs very straight for just over $^1/_2$ mile. As the track bends sharply to the right, look out for a barbed wire hook-on gateway on the left. Go through and across the meadow, veering towards the hedge on the right. Whistley Farm is ahead. Cross two small brooks on railway sleeper bridges, to reach Whistley Road at a farm gate. Cross over and follow a track on the near side of the farm buildings, which rises a little and bears left away from a field access gate, carrying on as a narrower path between thick hedges. There are occasional views of Potterne to the right and **Devizes** is reached through a wooded cutting, the road by now having become metalled.

Follow **Hartmoor Road,** cross Hillworth Road and head for St John's Church by way of a tarmac footpath and a footbridge over the dismantled railway line. Go left through ornamental gates into St John's Court, pass the Town Hall and reach Market Square by St John's Street. The Wharf car park can be reached by following Snuff Street and Couch Lane.

POINTS OF INTEREST:

Seend – Hilltop village, the rather unlikely site of a long defunct iron ore extraction industry and once a busy home-weaving centre of Flemish origin. Good parish church.
Devizes – Busy market town with excellent small museum, more than 500 listed buildings, and a particularly well-preserved market place.

REFRESHMENTS:

The Raven Inn, Poulshot (tel no: 0380 828271).
Devizes – any number of inns and restaurants; particularly famous is the *Bear Hotel*, once home of the painter Thomas Lawrence.

Walk 31   AROUND ASHTON KEYNES   9m (14.5km)

Maps: OS Sheets Landranger 163 & 173; Pathfinder SU 09/19.

A walk through farmland and gravel-workings.

Start: At 045942, the north-west corner of Ashton Keynes.

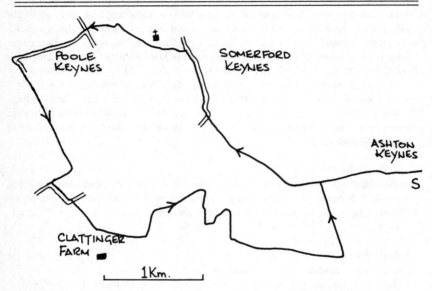

Set off along Church Walk and should you wish to visit **Ashton Keynes Church** cross the stream (which is, in fact, the Thames) and follow the avenue of chestnut trees. Otherwise keep to the left side of the stream, following the footpath as it leads beyond the houses. Cross over a road and continue in the same direction. Pass Culli's Bridge and **gravel workings** on left and right and continue until the path turns right over the stream. Turn left along the track, passing a lake on the right to reach a road. Cross over and walk up the cul-de-sac opposite, bearing right at the first T-junction. The Baker's Arms pub is on the left, about $\frac{1}{2}$ mile further on. About 50 yards beyond the pub, in front of the long, stone building with a 'Church Notices' sign, turn left down a gravel drive. At the end of the drive, turn right on a footpath which leads to **Somerford Keynes Church**.

From the edge of the churchyard follow the footpath, signed 'Poole Keynes', passing the beautiful old manor house. Climb the stile ahead and cross the footbridge. Bear right across the next field to a gate in the opposite hedge, then skirt the left edge of the field to reach farm buildings. Cross the bridge near the farm and bear right down the drive. At the crossroads continue straight on down the lane. Turn left at the grass triangle near Poole Keynes and pass farm buildings. Where the road bends left, go through a gate ahead. Cross the field, keeping to the left of the pylons, and go through a gate ahead. Bear left to join the hedge and go through a gate in front and go over a stile, right. Continue to the next stile and cross the field beyond, to the house opposite. Go down the drive, passing traction engines and fairground organs and turn left at the road.

Take the turning on the right to Clattinger Farm and follow the track towards a white gate. Bear left before the gate, following signs to Ashton Keynes. The path leads round two sides of a lake, then bears right across a field to the road. Cross the road to the gravel-pit area and follow the path beside the left-hand hedge. The footpath has been surfaced and is easy to follow. After passing an old barn on the left, cross the ditch and turn right down the track beyond. Turning left to the lake, bear right and make for the far-right corner of the long field. Go through a gap in the hedge and over a stile ahead. Continue straight across the next field to the opposite hedge, and, staying inside the field, turn left to follow the right-hand hedge. At the far end of the lake, go over a stile and turn right along the footpath back to the start.

POINTS OF INTEREST:

Ashton Keynes Church – A Norman chancel arch and font still remain. There are remains of a monastery adjoining the churchyard, surrounded by a moat and now converted into a farmhouse.

Gravel workings – This area provides an interesting example of a landscape in transition. Since it was discovered to be a valuable source of gravel, the farmland has been quarried away and a number of deep pits formed. When quarrying ceases these are flooded and put to a variety of uses. Some have been turned into nature reserves while others form the Cotswold Water Park.

Somerford Keynes Church – The original church dates from 700 AD, though most of what we see is 13th century. The small narrow doorway opposite the main entrance is Saxon.

REFRESHMENTS:
The Bakers Arms, Somerford Keynes (tel no: 0285 861298).

Walks 32 and 33   **BISHOPS CANNINGS**   11$\frac{1}{2}$m (18.5km)
Maps: OS Sheets Landranger 173; Pathfinder SU 06/16.
A walk along the Vale of Pewsey.
Start: At 037640, just off the A361 in the village of Bishops
Cannings. Patrons may park at The Crown Inn.

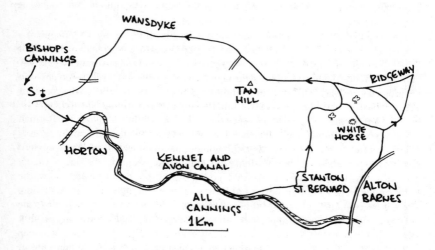

Leaving the Crown car park, turn right along the village road and take the footpath
through the churchyard next to the pub. Beyond the churchyard the path passes between
houses on Church Walk. At a road signposted 'Horton', go right. Where the road bends
right to go to Court Farm, go straight ahead on a footpath along a private farm road
(concrete). Pass through the Caravan Club touring-caravan site and cross a swingbridge
over the Kennet and Avon canal, continuing straight on along a double grassy track
between hedges. Another footpath goes off right but you keep straight on. The path
opens out and goes across a field towards a farm. Go over a stile at the corner of the
fence, cross a paddock and pass between a barn and Horton Mill Farm house, going
down a concrete farm drive to join a road. Go left and through Horton village. Before
the bridge over the canal, go right along the canal towpath. This is a beautifully kept

path with very pretty banks, a lot of wildlife (butterflies, waterfowl, heron) and a profusion of flowers. Pass the disused swingbridge, go under the next bridge and pass a dismantled bridge and foot swingbridge. At the next bridge over the canal, *either* go right through a small gate and along a double track across a field to visit All Cannings (a Best Kept Village with a good, friendly pub, the Kings Arms Inn) before rejoining the route, *or* continue along the towpath. At the next bridge, of brick, go up to and across a bridge to the other side of the canal. Just beyond the bridge, go right through a gateway and follow the obvious path around the edge of the fields, fence on right, at first parallel to the canal but then veering away left. From behind the farm buildings, leave the field and go right along a tarmac road. The road bends left by Pewsey Vale Riding Centre and then on through Stanton St Bernard village. Pass a cul-de-sac on the left and take the next turning left. The road bends sharp left after 75 yards. At the main road, go right for 100 yards, keeping to the wide grass verge. Cross the road and go through a gateway to follow a fence left. Go straight on through the next gateway and further on cross an unsurfaced farm track, still straight on (buildings along track to right). In the corner of a field at the foot of the hill, cross a stile into **Pewsey Down National Nature Reserve**.

Go left keeping parallel to the fence on the left but slightly above it. Go through a gateway almost immediately, then continue around the hillside along narrow, grassy 'sheep-tracks'. In the corner of the field, without passing through the gateway, turn right up this fenceline. Keeping the fence left, climb quite steeply up the side of a deep/narrow valley. In the corner of this field, go left over a stile by a gate and follow the fence on the right with trees beyond it. Pass a hunting gate into this tree plantation. There is a gate in the corner, but continue around the corner and along the fence to the next gate. Now, *either* go through the centre gate and straight ahead to the top of **Milk Hill**, *or* go through the further gate/stile, follow a fence right around the head of a steep valley and join an unsealed track leading to the Wansdyke (see * later). When a line of trees appears ahead, turn right at right-angles to reach a hunting gate in a fence above the hillside. There are spectacular views over the Vale of Pewsey from here. Go through the gate and diagonally left downhill to a stile by the next hunting gate. Go straight on to reach Alton Barnes White Horse, fenced around and almost unrecognisable from such close quarters! Keep above the White Horse and follow the obvious, narrow path on across the slope to the hill beyond. Around the spur of the hill, Adam's Grave is visible atop the next rise. The path drops down, crosses a small ditch/mound and rises again to visit Adam's Grave – a commanding viewpoint. Return to the ditch/mound and go right towards a road. Go up a bank to cross a stile on to the road and go left along it.

Go over a stile by a farm gate on the left, opposite a very broad double track. Now, *either* (for especially keen archaeologists!) go diagonally right along the ancient Ridgeway, first across a field to pass between a wood and farm, then along a well-defined track gradually uphill to reach **The Wansdyke** under the trees. Go left along the Wansdyke. The first $^1/_4$ mile may be overgrown, so go in the field alongside. *Or,* follow the fenceline on the left – could be muddy for a little way, but easily avoidable – passing a wood on the right. Continue steadily uphill and through a gate. Go through a second gate by some small trees, still following the fence on the left to the top of the rise. Cross the Wansdyke – a gap in the huge mound – (longer option joins here). Then go left and over a stile by a gate to follow the Wansdyke west.

The route stays along the Wansdyke, sometimes on the right of the ditch, sometimes along the top of the mound, with occasional stiles to cross fences, but is always clear. At an unsealed farm road (*) – escape route left along it to Stanton St Bernard – the Wansdyke begins climbing gradually and bends to the right, passing below the summit of Tan Hill on left (equal in height to Milk Hill). Cross a part-tarmac, part-unsealed track (emergency descent: left along track to Allington). From here, a double, unsurfaced farm track follows parallel to the Wansdyke on the right of it – walk along the track until it ends some way on, at farm buildings right on the Wansdyke. Go round to the right of the buildings and rejoin the top of the Wansdyke mound. Cross the muddy double track with a stile either side. At a double hardcore track, climb a stile on to the track – the Wansdyke continues west beyond a few stunted trees. Go left along the track, over the brow of a slight rise and pass a group of farm buildings on the right. Go gently downhill with the spire of Bishops Cannings church visible ahead.

Pass through the yard of Easton Farm and beyond the house turn right on to a tarmac road, then immediately left over a stile on to a path signposted 'Bourton/Bishops Cannings' (for Bishops Cannings see Walk 21). Go straight across the pasture to a stile, opposite the end of the hedge. Go on again with the hedge left. Go over stile/footbridge/stile under trees into the next field. Go over stile/footbridge and then go right around the edge of a field, past the back of some buildings and paddocks. At a stile behind a thatched cottage, put your back to the stile and go out across the field towards the village. Go over a footbridge and stile, then turn right along the edge of a field, towards the steeple. Before the corner go through a narrow gate to join a track alongside buildings. Go left to reach a road, cross it and go straight on along Church Walk retracing your steps at the start of the walk, to the Crown car park.

POINTS OF INTEREST:

Pewsey Downs National Nature Reserve – A landscape that is unspoiled, natural downland, never having been under the plough as has so much of the rest of the local countryside. Threatened species of native flowers and butterflies thrive in the protected environment – take a pocket handbook to identify what you see.

Milk Hill – A broad, flat, very exposed hill-top, the highest in Wiltshire at 964ft.

The Wansdyke – Dating from the 6th or 7th century, this huge earthwork was built by the ancient Britons as a defence against Saxons invading from the North. It was clearly successful as no pagan Saxon burials have been found south of here. Where the Ridgeway – older than the Wansdyke and Adam's Grave, and probably the oldest road in Europe – crosses the Wansdyke, was once an important place: the main trading route of the time crossing the frontier between two kingdoms – a kind of Checkpoint Charlie.

REFRESHMENTS:
The Crown Inn, Bishops Cannings (tel no: 0380 860218).
The Kings Arms Inn, All Cannings (tel no: 0380 860328).
The Barge Inn, Alton Barnes (tel no: 067285 238).

Walk 34   MILDENHALL AND THE RIVER KENNET   3m (5km)

Maps: OS Sheets Landranger 174; Pathfinder SU 26/36.

A short but quite energetic walk.

Start: At 213698, the village hall in Mildenhall.

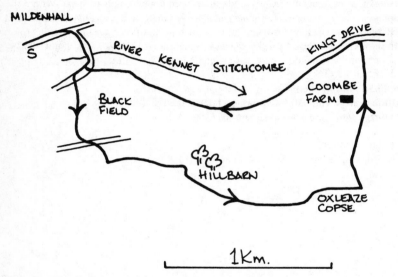

Follow the road towards Ramsbury until a right-turn leads to a bridge over the River Kennet. Follow the lane uphill to a T-junction. Turn left and in a very short distance slant right up the drive across the front of a bungalow. On passing the bungalow carry on uphill on a good path. This is Cock-a-troop Lane. By the corner of a small wood look for a gateless opening on the left and follow an ill-defined path by the hedge, with good views over the Kennet valley. In about 600 yards, Hill Barn is reached amongst woodland. Turn right and follow the farm track between the two buildings. Immediately beyond the open gateway turn left and stride over the low fence. Follow the hedgerow and large trees. The route here is over very rough grass. After striding over another low fence a metalled road is reached and crossed. Again the hedge is kept on the left. On reaching Oxleaze Copse carry on to the far end, looking carefully for a solitary gate post on the left with a stile a few yards behind.

Turn left into a lane beyond the stile and carry on downhill by Coombe Farm, forking right at the bottom edge of the wood. On reaching a metalled road (Kings Drive) turn left along the road for a short distance. As the road turns sharply left carry straight on over a stile and cross a small field to a stile on the far side. Cross the Stitchcombe road and follow a path signposted 'Werg' along the side of the river. This section of the route keeps close to the river, but generally a little way from the actual bank as the landowners try to keep this exclusive to anglers. As the river bends to the right, a stile will be seen on the left. Cross this and continue by a lightly used path near the hedge. On the left is the Blackfield, site of the Roman town of Cunetio. A stile is reached leading into the metalled road. Turn right and return to **Mildenhall** village hall.

POINTS OF INTEREST:
Mildenhall – The name is pronounced Minal. The village has attractive thatched houses, a shop, and a fine church with gallery and high box pews.

REFRESHMENTS:
The Horseshoe Inn, Mildenhall (tel no: 0672 54725).

Walk 35   **THE LYDIARDS** $3^{1}/_{2}$m (6km)

Maps: OS Sheets Landranger 173; Pathfinder SU 08/18.

This short walk follows footpaths through farmland.

Start: At 104847, the car park by the church in Lydiard Park.

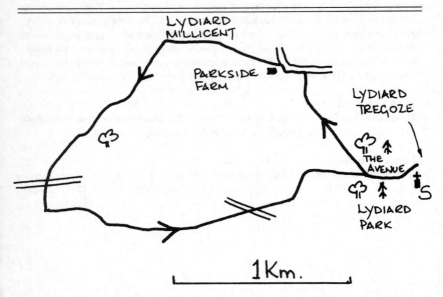

Before starting the walk consider visiting **Lydiard Tregoze Church**. From the car park, take the main path towards the conference centre, then follow signs to 'Visitor Centre' and 'Cafeteria'. Turn right at the main avenue leading away from the house following the sign to 'Farmland Walk'. At a crossing of tracks, continue straight on and look for the stile on the left, half concealed by trees. Climb the stile and head across the field towards a stile near the far right fence. Instead of climbing this stile, bear left following the fence. At the end of a narrow enclosure on the right, climb the stile, right, and head for a gate on the far side of the field. Cross the road and go through the gate opposite. Bear right through another gate and cross the field to its far left corner. Go through a gate and follow the hedge on the left to a stile. Climb the stile and cross the gully. Climb over the fence rails in the hedge, right. Follow the right-hand hedge into the next field and go through the first gate on the right, crossing the field towards a stile.

Go through the gate opposite and cross the field to the stile just beyond the water trough. Follow the right-hand hedge through the gate at the end of the field, then go through the gate immediately on the right. Bear left across the field, keeping to the right of the disused windpump, and following a faint track in the grass. Head for the gate opposite and cross the stream by the footbridge. In the next field bear right, heading just to the left of the two trees in the right-hand hedgerow and enter the field beyond. Bear left, cutting diagonally across the field to the far left corner. Go over the stile and follow the hedge on the left to reach a gate on the left. There is a good view of **Lydiard Millicent Church**. If you wish to visit the church, go through the gate and follow the left-hand hedge to a track which leads past the village hall.

Otherwise, pass in front of the gate and continue to follow the left-hand fence. Go through a gate into the next field and bear right towards the beautiful, old farmhouse on the other side. Pass in front of the farm and through a gate to reach a track which runs to the right beside the hay barn. Turn left beyond the gate. After a few yards climb a stile on the right and follow the path to a footbridge. Bear right across the field to another stile, then turn left, following the signpost to Lydiard Park (see Walk 25). From here the path is very well marked; continue ahead mainly following the hedge/fence, left, until you reach the trees surrounding Lydiard Park. Climb the stile, and continue straight on along the path to the main avenue. From here retrace your steps to the car park.

POINTS OF INTEREST:
Lydiard Tregoze Church – This beautiful little church is full of interesting monuments, though you will have to collect the key from the caretaker of the house to look inside. The gilded statue known as 'the Golden Cavalier' is of Edward St John, who died in 1645; the scene of his military exploits is carved on the pedestal. Also worth noting is the medieval glass in the windows and the Caroline window thought to be by Van Dyke. **Lydiard Millicent Church** – This pretty church has a Norman font and stoup and traces of ancient lancet windows.

REFRESHMENTS:
Several at Lydiard Tregoze and Lydiard Millicent

Walk 36   GREAT BEDWYN AND THE BRAILS   3¹/₂m (6km)

Maps: OS Sheets Landranger 174; Pathfinder SU 26/36.
An easy walk along a canal towpath and through woods.
Start: At 277643, in Church Street, Great Bedwyn.

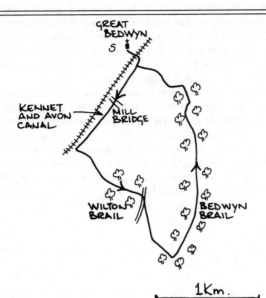

Just beyond the church in **Great Bedwyn** is a signpost to Bedwyn Brail. Take this path, going through a kissing gate into an extension of the churchyard. Go through a narrow V-stile into a field. Walk straight across and you will come to two kissing gates which take you over the railway (this is very much in use, so watch out for any trains) and then to the Kennet and Avon Canal and the River Dun. Cross the bridge and turn right, past a lock and follow the towpath for about ³/₄ mile, going underneath a bridge. When you come to a second bridge (Mill Bridge) and a lock, turn left, go through a gate and into a field. Walk along the right side of the field towards a wood ahead (Wilton Brail). At the edge of the wood there are footpaths signed both to the left and straight ahead. Go through a V-stile into the wood and walk straight ahead for a few yards until you come to a grass drive. Bear left and walk along the drive (which has some lovely wild flowers growing at its edges). The drive joins a hard-core path after a while. When you come

84

to a lane turn right into the lane and walk along it for a few yards. Turn left through some wooden gateposts on to a grass path. Here you can see Wilton Windmill about $1/_4$ mile to your right. The path, which has some good blackberries in the season, forks and you bear left, passing a pond on your left and a pit on the right. Follow the path up a slight incline, past a small turning into the wood, until you come to a farm track. Here, turn left into the wood which is signposted Bedwyn Brail (it also states that dogs must be kept on leads). Walk along a hard-core path through Bedwyn Brail for about 1 mile in all (you may see deer), at one point crossing the grass drive which you had been walking along earlier. If you look left down the drive, you can just make out a monument on the skyline, which is some 4 miles away at the edge of Savernake Forest. Keep straight on and when the track forks, bear left keeping to the hard-core. Eventually the road peters out into a grassy path in a large clearing. Continue straight on, then just as you come into some more trees turn left on to a narrow path. Follow this for about 100 yards until you come to a field at the end of the wood. Go through a V-stile and make for the far left of the field in front of you. Go over a stile into another field, and you can now see the village of Great Bedwyn ahead. Continue along the left side of the field down a small hill until you come to the canal and lock, where you started the walk. Retrace your steps over the bridge and the railway, through the churchyard and back to Church Street.

POINTS OF INTEREST:
Great Bedwyn – The church of St Mary the Virgin is built entirely of flint. The nave and the chancel are the oldest parts and date from the late 12th century.

REFRESHMENTS:
The Cross Keys (tel no: 0672 870678), in the middle of the village, serves simple, inexpensive food with very generous portions.

Walk 37   **RAMSBURY AND LITTLECOTE**   3³/₄m (6km)

Maps: OS Sheets Landranger 174; Pathfinder SU 27/37.

An easy to follow circuit all on very good tracks.

Start: Outside the Bell Inn at Ramsbury, site of the much-lamented ancient tree.

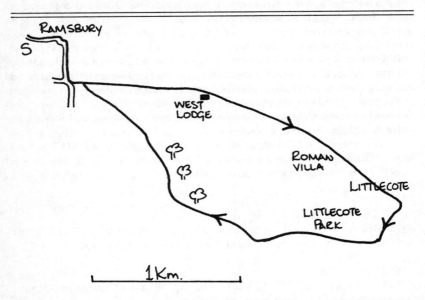

Proceed down the road towards Chilton Foliat, turning right at the Froxfield road to cross the River Kennet, most attractive at this point. In a short distance leave the road at farm buildings taking a broad trackway to the left signposted 'Littlecote House'. Keep left at a junction just beyond the farm buildings, following the line of the river. On reaching West Lodge, carry on, with the river now closer. At a junction of paths bear right, and look out for deer in the woodland on the left. The grounds of **Littlecote House** are soon reached. There is no Right of Way across these grounds, unless you pay the admission fee, but the remains of the comparatively recently discovered Roman villa may be seen very clearly from the track.

On reaching the two entry kiosks, turn right along the Littlecote approach road, past a timber and thatch house, heading for a belt of woodland. As the road bends left, turn right at a 'No Through Road' sign, and proceed slightly uphill, looking out again for deer and pheasants. At two ensuing junctions, bear right on each occasion. The countryside is now particularly attractive. As the track climbs steadily look out for a narrow footpath on the left plunging into the trees, with a public bridleway disc sign. Follow this delightful track downwards through the woods, with Ramsbury coming into view across the valley. Rejoin the original track at the farm buildings and turn right at the road to return to **Ramsbury**.

POINTS OF INTEREST:

Littlecote House – Elizabethan stately home with notable collection of armour, Roman villa remains, and other attractions for visitors. Exhibitions of jousting, and falconry. Also craft workshops, added by the present owner. For hours of opening and other details, telephone 0488 84000.

Ramsbury – Large village with many thatched cottages and other good buildings. The impressive church has Saxon remains.

REFRESHMENTS:

The Bell Inn, Ramsbury (tel no: 0672 20230).

AROUND WILTON   4m (6.5km)

Maps: OS Sheets Landranger 174; Pathfinder SU 26/36.

A short pleasant walk through woodland and by a canal.

Start: At the Swan Inn, Wilton.

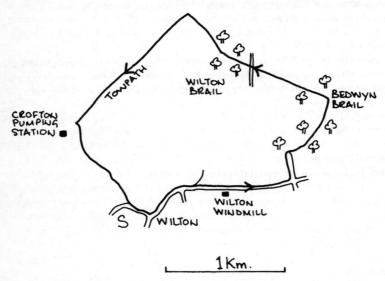

From the Swan follow the main street in the direction of Great Bedwyn (see Walk 36), and, after leaving the village, take the second turning on the right, signposted to Shalbourne and the windmill. The track leading to Wilton Windmill is about $^1/_4$ mile along this road on the right.

Continue past the windmill to the next turning on the right signposted to Marten. Turn left here down a grassy track and after a short distance pass through a gap in the fence to follow the track beneath the trees. At the first fork, turn right and continue to bear right when you reach the clearing on the left. A wide track leads from the gate which soon becomes visible to the left. Pass to the right of the gate and follow the track for $^1/_4$ mile, passing pheasant enclosures on the left. As a clearing opens out in the trees to the right allowing views of the countryside beyond, take the broad, grassy track to left. As you do so, Tottenham House, an imposing country house, now a prep school, is just visible in the distance. At the edge of the wood, climb the stile and cross the field to the gate opposite. Cross the road beyond and continue straight on along the track through Wilton Brail, heading in the same direction until you reach the edge of the wood. Cross a stile in the trees to the right at the bottom of the grassy slope. Cross the field beyond, keeping the fence on your left, to the gate beside the canal towpath. Turn left along the towpath and follow the course of the canal until you cross a track near a level crossing. Just beyond here, on the other side of the canal, is the **Crofton Pumping Station**, a working museum which is well worth a visit. It can be reached by crossing the canal at the next lock.

Just before the lock by the pumping station, take the path to the left signed to **Wilton Windmill**. The path follows the course of Wilton Water and takes you back to the road running through Wilton. Turn left to return to the Swan Inn.

POINTS OF INTEREST:

Wilton Windmill – The windmill can be viewed from the outside at all times and is open on Sundays and Bank Holidays from Easter to the end of September. The sails no longer turn, but there are interesting displays on the windmill's usage.

Crofton Pumping Station – At this fascinating working museum it is possible to see the oldest beam engine still capable of being operated. It was used to pump water into the Kennet Avon canal by means of steam power and the huge pistons and beams are an impressive sight. The museum is open every weekend from Easter to October, but the engine itself is operated only on occasional Bank Holiday weekends. Tel. no: 0672 870300, for information on operating times.

REFRESHMENTS:
The Swan Inn, Wilton (tel no: 0672 870274).

Walks 39, 40 and 41   **COATE WATER**   4m (6.5km)
Maps: OS Sheets Landranger 173; Pathfinder SU 08/18.
An easy walk mostly over well-made paths and level ground.
Longer (6m, 9.5km) and shorter (2m, 3.25km) are possible.
Start: At 177826, the car park at Coate Water Country Park.

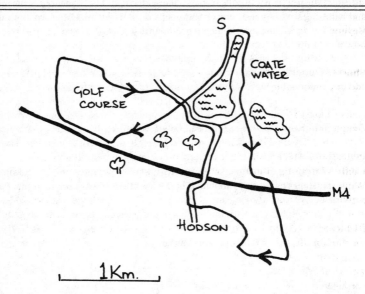

From the car park go through the entrance and left along a tarmac path to the lake. Go left around the lake. Pass toilets, left, and take a gravel path by a fence, left. Take the path that crosses the dam. At a signpost go right for the shorter, Lakeside Walk (*) or left for Hodson/Chisledon. At the end of the gravel track go over a stile and gate, and immediately right and over a second stile. Follow the hedge on the right towards the motorway. Before reaching the corner of the field, go over a double stile and then left to cross a spiral footbridge over the M4. Go left along an earth path. (This short section can be muddy.) Cross a stile by a gate and go diagonally right across a field to a stile into a small wood. Beyond the wood go right at the edge of a field with the hedge, right.

In the corner of the field continue ahead, on a path between trees and down into the valley. Go through a gate and down to cross the valley bottom. Go over a small stream and immediately turn right along the valley with the stream on your right. Go through a gate, and ahead with a wood on right. Half-way across the field go over stile and sleeper bridge on the right into wood. Go up between trees (rather overgrown), over a stile and at the top of the slope over another stile to leave the wood. Go left along the field edge. Follow the wood on the left to reach a road, but keep within the field to a stile just before a barn. Go over and right along the road. The road crosses the motorway and bends left, passes two houses and bends right. Here use the footpath to the right. Beyond trees cross a footbridge and go right, signposted ' Car park' (or **). There is now a well-defined gravel path back to **Coate Water** and the start.

Shorter/longer alternative routes: – For a shorter walk of 2m (3.25km) go right at (*) and circumnavigate the lake. The last part is as for the main walk.

For a longer walk of 6m (9.5km) go left at (**) and circle the Broome Manor golf course along an easily definable path, signposted 'Broome Manor Walk', before completing the last section of the main walk.

POINTS OF INTEREST:
Coate Water – Man-made lake, originally created as a reservoir for the now disused Wilts and Berks canal. It is now a large country park with many facilities for leisure activities.

REFRESHMENTS:
The Sun Inn (tel no: 0793 523292). Just off the Coate Water roundabout, next to the drive to the Park.
The Post House Hotel (tel no: 0793 524601). Opposite the Sun, across the dual carriageway.
The Spotted Cow (tel no: 0793 485832). A pub with a large children's play garden. A little further west along the dual carriageway.

There are plenty of opportunities for a wide variety of refreshments at Coate Water Country Park.

Walks 42 and 43 **CHERHILL DOWN** 4m (6.5km) or 5m (8km)
Maps: OS Sheets Landranger 173; Pathfinder SU 06/16.
A downland walk on grassy trackways.
Start: At 078692, a lay-by, near Beckhampton, on the A4 east of
Calne.

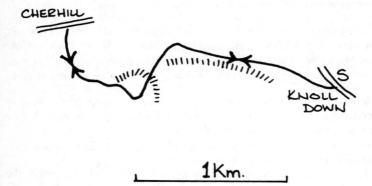

Walk to the end of the lay-by and pass through the trees towards a grassy track which
leads right towards a beech wood on higher ground. Keep to the track skirting the beech
copse on your right. Shortly, another track comes up from the left. Cross this and keep
straight on. (There are two tracks here, one to the right, broad and well-defined, one to
the left less clear – it does not matter which is followed.) Both the paths end at a gate
and stile. Cross the stile and follow the track with a fence right. (There are fine views
to the north and west here.) In about $1/_2$ mile the track begins to descend and changes
from grass to chalk. As the track descends further another chalky track comes up from
the main road below. Turn left on to this and gradually climb the downs towards another
beech wood on the right skyline. Soon a barnyard and gate is reached with another gate
and a stile on the right. Cross this stile and follow the track as it climbs uphill.

A 'National Trust' sign will be seen on the left of the track announcing Cherhill Down and Oldbury Castle. Climb the gate, which is difficult to open here, and in about 50 yards you may strike off right of the track and gain the mighty ditch and ramparts of the **Oldbury Castle**. Walking through the central part, **Lansdowne Memorial** will be seen in front.

On the north side of the obelisk it is possible, with care, to descend the downs and pick up the track seen below, which leads to the main road (A4). Turn left – the main road is today very quiet – for the Black Horse.

It is recommended that after visiting the obelisk and/or the pub, the walker returns by the same route to the car park near Beckhampton, for the views in this direction are perhaps even more spectacular than on the outward walk.

POINTS OF INTEREST:
Oldbury Castle – A prehistoric earthwork of majestic site.
Lansdowne Memorial – This stone obelisk commemorates Sir William Petty, a 17th-century economist, and was erected by the 3rd Marquis of Lansdowne, a descendant of Petty.

REFRESHMENTS:
The Black Horse, Cherhill (tel no: 0249 813365).
The Waggon and Horses, Beckhampton (tel no: 06723 262) (situated just past the Beckhampton roundabout on the A4 Marlborough road).

Walk 44   ALDBOURNE TO HILLDROP   4m (6.5km)

Maps: OS Sheets Landranger 174; Pathfinder SU 27/37.
An up and down walk partly on roads, but mainly on by-ways.
Start: The centre of the Aldbourne.

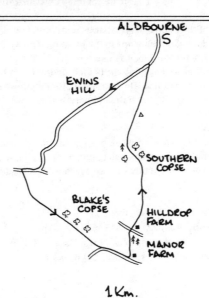

Cross the B4192 and proceed along Marlborough Road (signposted to Marlborough and Axford). After 100m leave the road, which turns right, and continue along The Butts, where there are some old thatched cottages. After passing the Sports Field the by-way continues uphill between high hedges. Where the by-ways diverge, take the right-hand one to Ewin's Hill. Where the hedge ends, there is a good view back to the village and along the B4192 with Liddington Camp on the far ridge. At the top of the hill you pass Ewin's Hill Farm on your right. The lane winds on through a wooded area and emerges on to the Ramsbury road. Turn right, passing the overgrown Laurel Pond. Shortly after this, turn left down a by-way to New Buildings, after which you pass through more woodland, with large oaks and cherry trees and lovely in spring.

The track emerges on to the Ramsbury-Marlborough road. Turn left down this. To the left can be seen Ramsbury and its church and to the right there are glimpses of

Ramsbury Manor through the tall beeches bordering the park. A Right of Way takes you to a bridge overlooking a lake with the Manor beyond. Retrace your steps to the Manor Farm where you turn along a bridleway. Shortly you come to a steep ascent beside a belt of woodland bordered, in spring, with primroses. Note the new conifer plantation at the top. Cross straight over the road at Hilldrop Farm and follow the by-way. After a short descent you cross another track and begin your last ascent, passing a new barn on the right. There has been more tree planting here, of hardwood trees. At the top the track veers right by the last stretch of woodland, which is unfenced. On the left are the remains of the wooded Aldbourne Common, which is a lovely sight in bluebell time and it is worth turning left to visit. To the right of the by-way is the site of a Roman building and a distant view of a range of downs which includes Inkpen Beacon. The last descent gives you a fine view of Aldbourne, old village and new estates nestling in the folds of the downs, dominated by the church.

POINTS OF INTEREST:
Ramsbury Manor – A fine 18th-century brick-built house with imposing iron gates.

REFRESHMENTS:
The Coffee Shop, Aldbourne, in the square.
The Blue Boar (tel no: 0672 40237).

Walk 45   **WHITESHARD BOTTOM**   4m (6.5km)

Maps: OS Sheets Landranger 174; Pathfinder SU 27/37.

A pleasantly varied walk with a long descent and a sharp ascent.

Start: At 238739, off Stock Lane from Aldbourne to Axford.

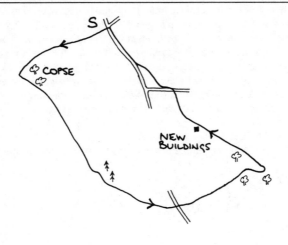

1 Km

The by-way, the oldest and most direct road to Marlborough, proceeds downhill between hedges. A gateway on the left affords a distant view of Martinsell, the highest point on the downs, above Pewsey Vale. The tall hedges are full of tits of all sorts, finches and goldcrests. In the spring look out for violets, bluebells and cowslips. At the bottom of the hill a track comes in from the right, but continue for another 50 yards and take a sharp turn to the left beside a small triangular spinney, unusual in having two Scots pines. Our track now goes along a valley between fenced hedges. Half-way along it becomes less well defined and nettles in summer can cause problems, but the great oaks and coppiced hazel are attractive. Eventually the path goes through open fields. Dogs must be on leads now, as there are often sheep grazing. The path comes out on to the Axford Road. If you have had enough of mud or nettles, turn left along the quiet road. An uphill walk of about 1 mile will bring you past Burney Farm, to your car.

If you are game for more adventure, cross straight over the road and follow the footpath sign, crossing a stile. Follow along the edge of a steeply ascending arable field, keeping left of the hedge. There is no real footpath here, though part of it is kept open by roe deer: look for their tracks. At the top, turn right through the wood for about 10 yards, then turn left and follow along the fenced edge of the field beside the wood. Leave the field by a short track which comes out to a by-way where you turn left, continuing past New Buildings, an old farm, to join the Hilldrop road to Ramsbury. Once past the wood there are wide views on the left over the Kennet Valley to the edge of Savernake Forest and thence to Martinsell. Turn left at the road. After about 100 yards there is a track on the right which skirts a wood, before coming on to the Axford road where you turn right. This track can be very muddy so you may prefer to stay on the road, turning right at the junction, where there is a fine clump of beech trees.

POINTS OF INTEREST:
This locality was once part of Aldbourne Chase. This, as part of the Manor of Aldbourne, became royal property under William I. Note the large oaks, dating back to the time when this was a hardwood forest and the coppiced hazels. These used to be cut back for making hurdles until World War II ended this practice, as sheep were no longer kept in folds.

Walk 46   OARE AND MARTINSELL HILL   4m (6.5km)

Maps: OS Sheets Landranger 173; Pathfinder SU 06/16.

A short and straightforward walk over attractive down.

Start: At 158631, in the village of Oare.

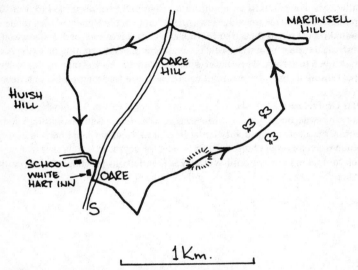

1 Km.

Cross the main road and proceed south-east along a metalled lane for a short distance, the surface soon becoming grassy. Rising to the left is a hill which appears to be more of a distinct peak than is usual in downland. This summit is our first objective. Immediately after another track comes in on the right, look out for a small gate on the left with a signpost 'Martinsell Hill'. Cross the field to another gate which is followed by a stile. The track now heads quite purposefully towards the peak. Climb steeply to the trig. point, by which time it will be obvious that our peak is merely the end of a prominent shoulder of the flat-topped upland of Martinsell Hill. After admiring the views of the Pewsey Vale and recovering breath, stride out on more level ground. The large house in the depression to the left is the late Georgian Rainscombe House. On reaching a gate, bear a little left, following a 'Martinsell' signpost. At the next gate turn left into a broad grassy trackway, noting a disc footpath sign. When this track bends sharply to the left, turn right and follow a rutted farm track along the edge of the woodland. The outer bank of Martinsell hill fort soon comes into view. Those walking in July may be rewarded by finding raspberries growing wild at one point on the woodland fringe.

Turn left to reach a signpost at the junction of four tracks. Although the hill fort generally comprises cultivated land, its boundaries may be explored. In the south-east corner there is a trig. point. Returning to the signpost, take the bridleway to Oare Hill, through the woodland. On reaching a farm track turn right and then go straight across the main road at the top of Oare Hill, following a 'public footpath and bridleway' sign. In $^1/_2$ mile at the near edge of a belt of woodland, look carefully for a somewhat overgrown track to the left. On reaching open meadow the track disappears. Bear to the left to find a route between two barbed wire fences, aiming down Huish Hill directly to **Oare** village.

Half-way down there is a seat placed in a strategic position. Below the seat, the faint path continues to the right of the fences. At the foot of an uncomfortably steep descent, there is a gate beyond which the ground levels and the path improves, leading to the metalled road by the school.

Turn left, then right at the main road, passing (or calling at) the White Hart Inn, before turning right again to reach the village hall.

POINTS OF INTEREST:
Oare – Oare House is a small mansion of 1740, with wings added in the 1920s by Clough Williams-Ellis of Portmeirion fame. The church is red-brick Victorian.

REFRESHMENTS:
The White Hart Inn, Oare (tel no: 0672 810336).

Walk 47   BUTTERMERE AND INKPEN HILL   4¹/₂m (7.5km)

Maps: OS Sheets Landranger 174; Pathfinder SU 26/36.

This walk covers some of the highest ground in Wiltshire as well as one of its quietest valleys.

Start: The tiny village of Buttermere.

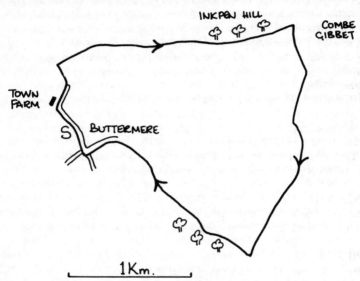

From the grass triangle at the northern edge of the village take the No Through Road past the farm and several houses. Once past the houses continue along the track beyond, bearing slightly left beside the trees. As you reach the edge of the hillside, a magnificent view opens up in front of you. Turn right at the bridleway and follow its course along the edge of the ridge. As you proceed, four counties become visible: Wiltshire in the immediate vicinity, Berkshire ahead and near left, Hampshire to the right and Oxfordshire to the distant left. The clump of beech trees on your left marks the border of Wiltshire with Berkshire. A short distance further on, look for **Combe Gibbet** on the hillside beyond. This can be reached by continuing straight on along the track.

As the path descends into a small valley, turn sharp right just after the clump of six beech trees on the right, following the public bridleway sign. Follow the path along the line of the right-hand hedge, looking to the left for a good view of **Walbury Hill**. The path continues between two fields, begins to descend into the valley, then veers left following the left-hand hedge. It then keeps to the left side of the beautiful, quiet valley without a building or a road in sight.

Follow the path as it leads between the woodland on the left and the fence on the right, and when the path bends left into an adjacent field continue straight on for another $^1/_4$ mile to a stile in the right-hand fence. Head straight across the field and down the hill, bearing slightly left past the corner of the small plantation and further left to the stile in the fence ahead. Make for the chalky track below and turn right, then continue along the right-hand side of the wood and up the valley. Continue to follow the track between fences along the valley bottom, then, near a dilapidated rail cart and a collapsed barn, follow the track past a large sycamore and beneath other trees. Pass tiny Buttermere Church on the left and continue up the road to the T-junction. Turn right past the telephone box and keep straight on back to the grass triangle.

POINTS OF INTEREST:

Combe Gibbet – The gibbet visible from the path has never been used, but is a replica of others which stood on the same spot. Legend links the gibbet to the Combe Wife-Killer, a man from the nearby village of Combe who pushed his shrewish wife into a dew pond so that he could marry his lover. Both husband and mistress were condemned to death and it is said that the bodies were displayed on the gibbet after their execution. Certainly the gibbet was standing in 1676, and since then others have been raised on the hill, visible for miles around. The gibbet stands on an ancient stone-age burial mound, used as a communal grave by the earliest farming communities here.

Walbury Hill – At 297m Walbury Hill is the highest point in the south-east of England and an obvious spot for the ancient hill fort which circles its summit. Walbury Camp is the largest iron-age hill fort in Berkshire, with a circumference of 1 mile.

REFRESHMENTS:
Available in Buttermere.

Walk 48   PIGS HILL AND MARRIDGE HILL   5m (8km)

Maps: OS Sheets Landranger 174; Pathfinder SU 27/37.
A varied walk with quite steep ascents and easy downhill stretches.
Start: At 264757, the centre of Aldbourne.

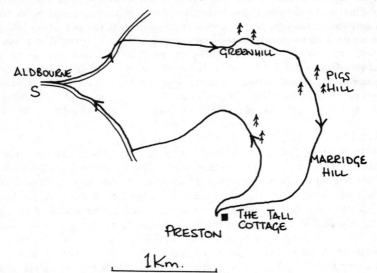

Leave the village on the Baydon road. A steep climb will take you to the brow of the
hill where you will find a footpath sign on the right-hand side of the road by Baydon
Hill Farm. Taking this path you will find that the first half is in the farmer's field and
should be easy going. You climb again to the top of the path which will bring you to
a junction with a by-way. This area is called Greenhill and there is a beautiful view of
Aldbourne. To your right and just below you there is an old copse – Peggy Knowl
Copse. Cross over the by-way and carry straight on with a copse, Greenhill Trees, on
your left. The path then becomes rather overgrown as you keep the hedgerow on your
left until you come to an open track with a long gentle descent. At the bottom you turn
right on to Pigs Hill. This is a long ascent with Pigs Hill Wood on the left-hand side.
At the top of the track the surface becomes metalled. This takes you to Marridge Hill,
a very pretty and quiet little hamlet.

Follow the road through Marridge Hill bearing right for Preston. This is a long and, at times, quite a steep descent with good views on the lower half. When you reach the bottom of the hill you will see a very pretty Toll Cottage on your left. Turn immediately right with the brook on your right. After 100 yards you cross the brook which, being fed by springs, is dry from the end of June until springtime. A long climb to the top of Green Hill follows, with Winchcombe Copse on your left. About 200 yards past the copse a junction on the left will take you downhill once more to join the B4192. Turn right and a short walk will take you back to the village centre. There is a pavement along this road to avoid the dangers of traffic.

REFRESHMENTS:
The Blue Boar, Aldbourne (tel no: 0672 40237).

Walk 49   WINDMILL HILL   5m (8km)

Maps: OS Sheets Landranger 173; Pathfinder SU 07/17.

A walk, for the most part, on level tracks.

Start: At 099733, in the village of Berwick Bassett.

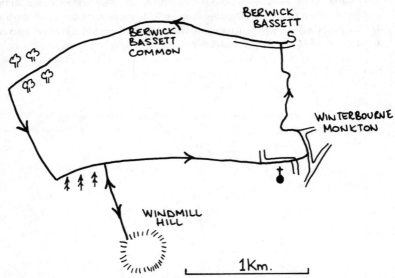

Walk up the lane to the left passing Berwick House Farm on the right. After $1/_4$ mile the lane becomes a farm track. Follow this track across pleasant open farmland for about $1^1/_2$ miles. The track eventually ends at the entrance to a field on the right. Continue forwards for about 50 yards, however, on a grassy track towards a hedge and trees. Here the grassy track turns left. In a few yards to the right there is a gap in the hedge. Turn right through this and follow a narrow, but well-trodden path, through the wood. This emerges into a field with a grass track to the left. Follow this track for about $1/_2$ mile as it gradually rises to higher ground. There are good views to the right towards Yatesbury, and Lansdowne Memorial Obelisk (see Walks 42/43) can be seen on the skyline. This part of the walk traverses the most remote stretch of countryside in the area, some distance from any road. On gaining the higher ground a conifer plantation will be seen on the left ahead. Turn left here at the signs welcoming considerate horse-riders. Walk along the gently descending track with the plantation on the right. In about $^1/_4$ mile a water tank will be seen with a well-defined crossroads of the farm track. Turn right at the water tank and go straight ahead with a hedge on your right. This path gradually ascends to **Windmill Hill**.

After visiting Windmill Hill retrace your steps down to the water tank and here turn right along the broad track which leads into the lane near Winterbourne Monkton Church. To continue, follow the lane past the church for a short distance and then follow the footpath to the left which leads to the village street. Turn left here. Continue down the village street to the left and where the lane turns right follow the signposted path across the field to Berwick Bassett, reached in about $^1/_2$ mile. On reaching the lane in Berwick turn right and a few steps return you to the village.

POINTS OF INTEREST:

Windmill Hill – Famous neolithic camp. There are several tumuli both within and outside the earthworks which form a fine vantage point around the whole area towards Avebury and the Pewsey Downs.

REFRESHMENTS:

The New Inn, Winterbourne Monkton (tel no: 06723 240).

Walk 50   AROUND BROAD HINTON   5m (8km)

Maps: OS Sheets Landranger 173; Pathfinder SU 07/17.

A walk mainly along village paths and quiet lanes.

Start: Broad Hinton church.

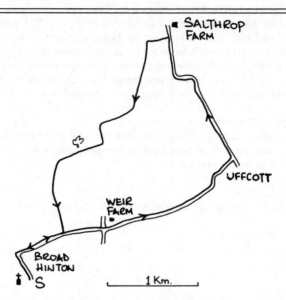

From the parking place left of the church walk across the field towards the gap in tall beech trees. Turn left along the farm track and keep left following the track in front of Broad Hinton House.

On reaching the main road just past the house, turn left for some 50 yards. Turn right down Post Office Lane and in about 100 yards take the left-hand lane to a bungalow. A pedestrian path leads to the right of the bungalow around the edge of a new estate with open fields to the right. This soon emerges opposite a large white bungalow. Cross the road and follow the path to the left of this bungalow. Continue through this small estate of large bungalows and houses (Fortunes Fields), keeping to the path until this ends at a T-junction with a lane.

Turn right and walk along the lane for almost $1/_2$ mile until a crossroads is reached. Cross the main A4361, passing Weir Farm on the left and continue along the lane, which reaches the village of Uffcott in about 1 mile. (There are wide views all around to the higher downland of Hackpen Hill and Barbury Castle.) Walk through the quiet and attractive village of Uffcott, keeping to the lane which turns sharp left after the village. Continue for about $^1/_2$ mile when another crossroads will be reached. Cross the main road and continue forwards (signposted 'Salthrop'). This lane bends right, left and then sharp left in about $^1/_2$ mile. Just before reaching a farm (Salthrop Farm) on the right, turn left down a farm track towards a large corrugated barn.

Continue along the track for about $^1/_4$ mile and another similar barn will be found. There is a signpost here. Follow the track forward to Broad Hinton ($1^1/_2$ miles). The track soon ends in a field where you bear right along the right edge of a field. At the top of the field turn left along the field edge to a gate where you turn right on to a grassy track. After about 300 yards go through a gate and turn left along the hedge. Bear half-right in this field towards a metal farm gate on the far side. Cross the track to another gate immediately opposite. Walk down this field with a fence right towards a small bungalow at the bottom. Turn right into the lane by the bungalow and follow it for about $^1/_4$ mile to a T-junction. Turn left here and walk past the Post Office/Village Shop. The Bell Inn is at the bottom end of Post Office Lane. The Crown is about 100 yards on the right. To return to the church continue forwards up the village street to The Well and the church will be seen past the three thatched cottages on the right.

POINTS OF INTEREST:
Broad Hinton House – This fine large Victorian house has attractive deep eaves and shell-woods to its windows.

REFRESHMENTS:
The Crown Inn, Broad Hinton (tel no: 079373 302).
The Bell Inn, Broad Hinton (tel no: 079373 251).

Walks 51 and 52   **ROCKLEY**   5m (8km)
Maps: OS Sheets Landranger 173; Pathfinder SU 07/17.
High downland walk over gentle, easy ground.
Start: At 158719, the crossroads in Rockley.

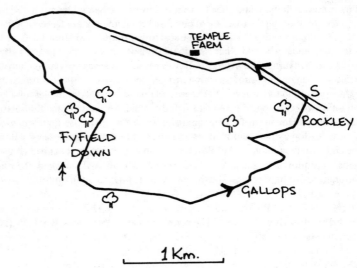

Set off along the private continuation of the road through the village (Public Bridleway to Temple Farm). The route continues up a broad, downland valley. Tarmac ends at Top Temple, but the track continues between house and buildings. Follow the flint track to the head of valley. Just beyond a small quarry the track merges with another coming in from the right. Keep ahead to a hunting gate at the head of the valley. This is the highest point of the walk. Go left through the gate and along a broad earth/grass track. At a T-junction with a hardcore track turn right along it and in 50 yards go left (signposted 'Manton Down'). This broad, grassy track follows the fence line on the left. There are numerous sarsen stones piled up along it, moved off the farm land. On reaching wood, continue ahead, between wood and hedge. Watch out for deer here. Pass through a hunting gate to reach the **Fyfield Down Nature Reserve**.

Go straight on, past a dew pond amongst bushes on right. At a field gate (*) do not go through, but turn right along a broad grassy track. Go through a field gate, or over the hunting rail, into Grey Wethers, where the scattered sarsen stones look like sheep – wethers – lying in the grass. Leaving the wood behind and keeping the fence to the left, walk down to a cottage amongst trees. Just past the cottage turn left over a stile, skirting the cottage garden. Cross a concreted sheep-yard to a track. Go left on this for 15 yards then right on to a grassy track. Keep the fence on your right and head towards the top corner of the wood ahead. From the corner go gently downhill. Go over a stile by a gate in the right corner of the field, and leave the Nature Reserve.

Continue ahead – out across the training gallops. Two-foot posts at 100 yards intervals indicate the route across this totally open downland. The marker posts lead to a signpost by a standing stone. Follow the route for **Rockley**, passing through a gate in a thick hedge and going straight over a road. The route now continues along a 20 yards wide grass strip. Cross a second road then go slightly to the left of a hedge, and keep the hedge to your right. At the end of the hedge cross another gallop in a gentle dip. **Manton House** can be seen up to your right. Go out of the dip to a signpost, cross another gallop and beyond it go left along a third road, dropping gently downhill. At the end of the road-side gallop, before passing a fence turn right and keep the fence on your left, following it back along a line of beech trees. By a gateway the track passes through the line of beech trees down into more trees. It broadens out, and takes you back to the start.

Shorter route – A shorter walk can easily be arranged by forming the rough loop of the route into a figure of eight. The central bar leads from the gate at (*****). Go through the gate and bear left, signposted Rockley/ Marlborough, down a shallow valley, straight back to the car at Rockley, the last $^3/_5$ mile.

POINTS OF INTEREST:

Fyfield Down Nature Reserve – One of the largest downland tracts containing sarsen stones in Britain. Actively conserved and farmed as it has been for many centuries. Here is true, traditional downland, with its attendant downland flora and fauna. Birds you may see include sparrowhawks, kestrels, long-eared owls, buzzards or even stone curlews or red kites.

Rockley – one of the few surviving true ancient hamlets in England, all the houses and land belonging to one owner.

Manton House –A very old and very large horse-racing training establishment, hence the numerous training gallops in the vicinity.

Walk 53   AROUND WINTERBOURNE BASSETT   5m (8km)

Maps: OS Sheets Landranger 173; Pathfinder SU 07/17.

A downland walk with wide views.

Start: The Bell Inn, Broad Hinton.

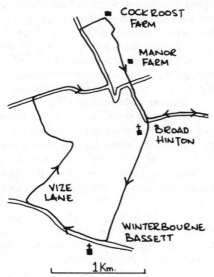

Cross the A4361 and go down Post Office Lane opposite. Follow the lane between houses for some $1/4$ mile, reaching a T-junction. Cross the road (B4041) towards two old thatched cottages where you turn left past some new housing. In a few yards there is a signpost by the church to Winterbourne Bassett. Follow this going across a field to reach a broad grassy path that stretches ahead for about 1 mile. (There are good views from here forward and left to the higher ground of the Marlborough Downs.) When the path reaches Winterbourne Bassett, turn left into a lane and in a few yards the White Horse is on the left. A few steps beyond is a signpost to the church across the lane on the right. Follow this, skirting the pond, and the fine setting of the church and manor house may be seen. Retrace your steps to the village street, turn left and carry on through the village. Follow the quiet lane for about $1/2$ mile. At the top of a short rise two signposts will be seen: take the right track marked 'By-Way to Broad Hinton', passing through a metal gate and following the track downhill. (There is a stone circle to the right of this track.) At the bottom of the descent there is another gate. Go through into a field, keeping along the left edge. The path climbs slightly to a further gate. Go through and about 100 yards another gate is reached. Carry on forwards and into a broad grassy track, Vize Lane, which runs ahead.

After passing through this last gate watch carefully on the left for a field entrance with a footpath disc on a gatepost. Pass through and walk along the left edge of the field; at the far side pass into the next field, steering towards a barn. Carry on forwards and in a short distance reach a metalled lane. Turn right and proceed for $^1/_2$ mile until the T-junction with two cottages left is reached. Turn left here and follow the road (B4041) for about $^1/_2$ mile. On the right look for a sign 'Hinton Holsteins'. Turn right down the track, to Cockroost Farm 200 yards ahead. The large farmhouse is hidden behind a conifer screen just after a sign 'Slow – Free Range Children'! Turn right just past this down a broad, grassy track which soon leads to a field. Go through the gate and keep left across the field. A plank footbridge will be found ahead: cross this and climb the fence/stile still keeping along the left edge of the field. Steer towards two dead elm trees and reach a farmyard pond at Manor Farm. Bear right here and cross the field towards **Broad Hinton** school ahead. On gaining the lane a few steps to the right lead to a T-junction. Turn left and go ahead down the village street. As the street bends left the top of Post Office Lane is reached for a return to the start.

POINTS OF INTEREST:

Broad Hinton Church – There is an interesting churchyard with some unusual iron and sarsen tombstones, while the interior of the church contains a fine monument to Sir Thomas Wroughton.

REFRESHMENTS:
The Bell Inn, Broad Hinton (tel no: 079373 251).
The Crown Inn, Broad Hinton (tel no: 079373 302).

Walk 54 STANTON FITZWARREN TO CASTLE HILL 5$\frac{1}{2}$m (9km)

Maps: OS Sheets Landranger 173; Pathfinder SU 09/19.

A walk through pleasant farmland and over high ground with good views.

Start: In the village of Stanton Fitzwarren.

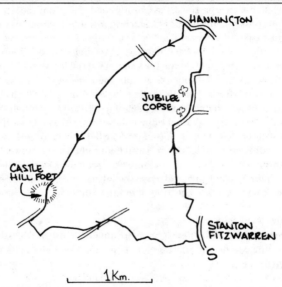

Walk from the junction with Mill Lane down the main street and out of the village. Then follow the footpath on the left signposted to Hannington. Cross the footbridge over the stream and turn right along the course of the disused railway. About 100 yards further on follow the left fork of the track between the fields, then, as you approach the farm, turn right down the drive towards the road. Turn left at the road and a short distance further on take the stony track on the right which, after a short while, becomes pleasant and grassy. Continue to follow this track uphill, ignoring the first turning on the left, bearing right, instead, through Jubilee Copse. As you near the top of the hill turn left and follow the track until you reach a gate straight ahead of you. Turn right just before the gate along a small track beneath trees which follows the right edge of the field. Eventually you will emerge in Hannington. Turn left down the main street of this quiet and pretty village. Pass the Jolly Tar pub on your left and just before the next turning on the right climb the stile on the left. Follow the little path leading between cottage gardens and into the field beyond. Climb the stile on the other side of the field, and turn right along the right-hand fence. Go through the gate at the end and head for a row of trees. The Right of Way continues on the other side of these trees but it has been blocked, so turn right along the track beneath the trees and go through the first gate on your left.

As you follow the right-hand fence down the hill, the views over the plain are spectacular. Go through the gate at the end of the field and continue down the track straight ahead. At the bottom of the field, bear left then right across the ditch. Go through the gate on the right, following the left-hand hedge and passing through the first gate on the left. Head for the gate on the opposite side of the field then continue in the same direction across the next field towards the oak tree in the far right-hand corner. Pass through the gate and proceed up the hill, keeping the hedge on your left. After the next gate, climb the fence on the right and bearing slightly right, head up Castle Hill to the fort at the top. At the top bear left towards the roof of the house just showing above the opposite rampart. Climb a stile and turn right along a lane. After a few hundred yards follow the footpath sign over an overgrown stile on the left and along the edge of the cemetery. Half-way along the hedge beyond, strike off left across the field to the metal gate on the other side. From here bear right to the stile at the far-right corner of the field, passing old gun emplacements on your left.

Turn left along the road and proceed for several hundred yards, until you pass the end of the field to the right of the road. Go through the gap in the hedge just before the white box on the right, and at the bottom of the field bear left along the line of willow trees to a gate and stile on the right. Cross the footbridge on the other side of the field and make for the gate at the far end of the left-hand hedge. Now follow the right-hand hedge to the end of the next field. Turn into the field on the right and take the track which runs left along the edge of this field and leads eventually to a kissing gate at the top of Mill Lane. Take this back to the start.

REFRESHMENTS:

The Jolly Tar, Hannington (tel no: 0793 762245). Has a large garden with climbing frames etc., and serves food.

Walk 55   **WROUGHTON AND CLOUTS WOOD**   5¹/₂m (9km)

Maps: OS Sheets Landranger 173; Pathfinder SU 07/17 & 08/18.

A walk along the edge of the downs with good views north.

Start: The small car park in Wroughton.

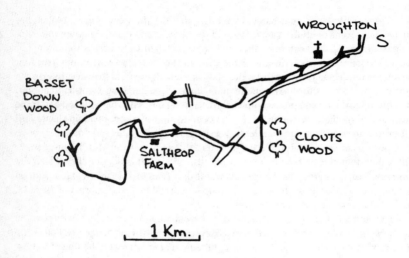

From the car park turn right into Wharf Road, and right again into the High Street. Go forwards up Church Hill passing the Carters Rest and the Fox and Hounds. On reaching the top of Church Hill take the right fork and pass the church. Keep straight ahead and enter the churchyard through the small gate. Follow this path as it gradually descends the hill and joins a meadow path beyond another gate. On the far side of the meadow turn left into a lane. Walk up the lane, ignoring the signpost on the right to The Kems. As the lane climbs it takes a sharp right hairpin. Opposite here take the signposted path across the hill to Basset Down. In just over 1 mile a metalled lane is reached. Cross over and take the path along the edge of Basset Down Wood (signposted Bincknoll Castle). There are good views right through the woods towards west Swindon and the Vale.

As the path starts to descend through the woods, keep up to the left through a gate and keep the railings on your right. Keep right through this large field until reaching a small copse. On the far side of the copse is a stile and signpost for **Bincknoll Castle**. Cross the stile and keep to the right edge of the field to reach a stile at the entrance of the large earthwork of the Castle.

Retrace your steps to the signpost at the copse. After re-crossing the stile walk straight forward ignoring the signpost to Broad Hinton. In a few yards a tufted path leads across the fields with a shallow ditch on the left. In about $^1/_2$ mile a large corrugated barn is reached. There is a signpost here to Basset Down. Turn left and follow this farm track. Soon a second barn is reached. Turn left just before this barn through a gap in the hedge and walk along the right-hand edge of the field. Follow the path past an overgrown copse, right, to reach a road. Turn right passing two white cottages left, to reaching a farm where the lane turns left. Take this left turn and follow the pleasant lane across open downland for about $^3/_4$ mile, passing the 208m triangulation point on the left. In a short distance the main A4361 is reached. Cross this road very carefully and follow the signpost opposite to Clouts Wood. This path descends the hill on the right of the field. At the bottom, on the edge of the wood, the path turns left and in $^1/_2$ mile emerges on to the main road. Turn right for the start.

POINTS OF INTEREST:

Bincknoll Castle – An expansive Iron Age hill fort with fine views from its central area.

REFRESHMENTS:

The Fox and Hounds, Church Hill, Wroughton (tel no: 0793 812217).
The Carters Rest, Church Hill, Wroughton (tel no: 0793 812288).
Wroughton is blessed with a plethora of pubs, but these two are the nearest!

Walk 56   **SUGAR HILL AND LIDDINGTON**   5¹/₂m (9km)
Maps: OS Sheets Landranger 174; Pathfinder SU 27/37 & 28/38.
An easy walk over high ground with fine views.
Start: At 230786, a lay-by on the B4192, two miles south-east of
Liddington.

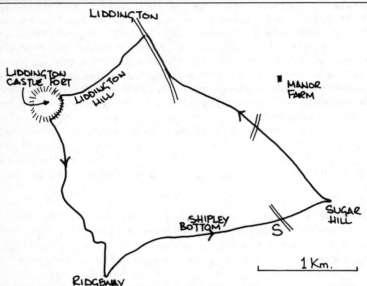

Walk to the end of the avenue then turn left off the road following the wide, grassy track
signed 'By-way to Peaks Down'. This is the only steep ascent of the walk and you will
be rewarded by some fine views of Shipley Bottom which lies behind you. At the top
of the hill climb the stile beside the left-hand gate and follow the fence to your left. From
here walk the entire length of the ridge, always keeping the fence on your left. Where
the main track bends right towards Manor Farm, continue straight on, up the grassy
track ahead, following the line of small hawthorn trees. After reaching the field which
borders the B4192, head for the small metal gate at the diagonally opposite corner of
the field. Go over to a path which follows the course of the road in the direction of
Swindon. Look out for a sign on your left marked 'Aldbourne'. Go over the stile and
cross the road. A stony track leads away from the road, straight up to the summit of

116

Liddington Hill. At the gate near the brow of the hill head towards the clump of trees to your right, keeping the fence on your right side. Climb the stile in front of you and follow the hedge round to the left. The trees and the old gun emplacement can be most easily reached from this side. With spectacular views of Swindon to your right, continue to follow the line of the fence on your left until you reach **Liddington Castle**. At this point you may wish to climb the ramparts to the trig. point and explore the circle of earthworks. The views are magnificent and in summer the turf is studded with wild flowers.

Proceed along the path between the trig. point and the nearby fence until you leave the fort behind you. The view from here across the valley to the Marlborough Downs is spectacular: you can just make out the White Horse at Hackpen. Continue to follow the line of the fence on your left until you reach a broad grassy track, which comes up behind. Follow this uphill and through the gate on the horizon, then follow the line of the hedge to your left until you reach a stile at the end of the field. Climb the stile and turn right on to the **Ridgeway**.

When you see another stile on the right, double back to the left along a grassy track leading downhill to Shipley Bottom. You should now be able to see the avenue of trees where you left the car. The path will take you back to it. On the way down look out for the many wild flowers in the grass verges.

POINTS OF INTEREST:
Liddington Hill – The clump of trees on the top of Liddington Hill is a distinctive landmark that can be seen for miles around. It was a favourite destination for Richard Jefferies, the 19th-century chronicler of rural life who lived at nearby Coate Water.
Liddington Castle – The deep ditch and ramparts surrounding the summit of the hill are the remains of one of a string of hill forts on the northern edge of the downs. Its tactical position on the summit of Liddington Hill means that it commands superb views of the surrounding countryside.
Ridgeway – Thought to be one of the oldest roads in the country, the Ridgeway runs from Overton Hill, near Avebury, to Ivinghoe Beacon, Buckinghamshire, a distance of some 85 miles.

REFRESHMENTS:
The Blue Boar, Aldbourne (tel no: 0672 40237) is right on the village green and is simple and unpretentious with a choice of basic food.
The Crown, Aldbourne (tel no: 0672 40214) has a rather more sophisticated menu.

Maps: OS Sheets Landranger 173; Pathfinder SU 08/18.

A very easy walk with virtually no hills.

Start: At 131838, the car park behind the Queensway and Texas superstores.

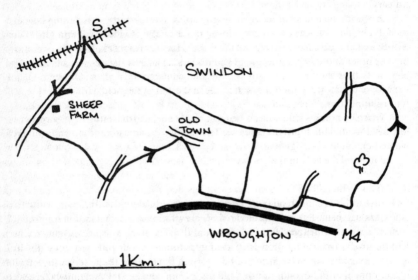

The route explores a unique area of countryside which has remained virtually unchanged despite its position between Old Town, Swindon and the M4 motorway.

From the car park go left and turn left along road to Southleaze, passing under the main railway line. Continue along a narrow, tarmac lane – a private road and public footpath – between farm fields with the railway to the right. At the first farm on the left, stop to visit the **Sheep Milking Parlour**, farm and shop. In about 100 yards, well before the large farm on the right, go left over a stile signed 'Wroughton' and then through a farm gate just ahead. Walk straight across the middle of this large field to a stile in the fence on the far side. Again go across the next, small field and over a footbridge with a stile at either side. The following field is also small – go straight across it and over a double stile beneath trees. All these fields are likely to have sheep in them – please keep dogs under total control. After the double stile, set off bearing slightly right across a field to the gateway on a raised mound astride a dip (the remains of the old Wilts and Berks canal). Continue in the same direction, slightly to the right, to a stile. Go across this last field and up the zigzag path on to a broad lane by a signpost. Go left along the tarmac lane, using the grass verge, for about 100 yards then cross over and go through a farm gate by a signpost. Go half left across the field, over a stile, and continue in the same direction to the corner of the next field. Go through a gateway in the fence on the left and then with the hedge on the right, go towards the brick cottage (boarding kennels). Old Town and Princess Margaret Hospital are on the skyline and **The Old Town Railway Line** path (for the return half of the walk) passes just below. Go over a stile in the corner of the field by a signpost, join a tarmac lane by the kennels and turn right. Cross the bridge over a small stream by a bungalow on the right and go immediately right over a stile, signed 'Wroughton'. Keep to the fence/hedge line for the next $\frac{1}{2}$ mile via a double stile over a small weir, alongside the M4, a stile in a corner by some bushes and a marshy pond, a stile under a hedge, around the base of a ramp to a footpath over the M4 (*, but do not turn off here) a stile and finally over a double stile and out on to a dead-end lane by a signpost.

Go left – the only option! – past the veterinary clinic, a house and two bungalows on the left. Just before the lane meets a main road at a T-junction, go left along a pavement. Where the pavement comes alongside a road (before houses at the bottom of a hill), cross over the road (***with care***) to join an unsealed path following a ditch and some houses on the left. Further along, there are allotments beyond the ditch and hedge. At a T-junction with a road (Old Town by-pass) go left along a tarmac pavement which crosses over a ditch and follows the allotments round. About 100 yards after the ditch go left along an unsealed path before a development, to follow the hedge on the left with the allotments still beyond. At a vehicle track from between the bungalows (access to the allotments) keep on along the unsealed path with the hedge and then woods on the left. The path turns left into a wood and goes uphill. The wood, Great Copse, is a haze of blue in April/May when the bluebells are in bloom. About half-way up the hill, turn off left through the woods with houses and then a playing field bordering the woods on the left, the Intel office block bordering on the right. Find the path which leaves the woods between the Intel office block and the Holiday Inn hotel, a gravel track fenced on both sides. Come out at a roundabout and go left passing the hotel entrance road, and carry on to the pavement. Cross over a road when the pavement ends and go on to a grassy slope leading up to a bridge over a street (dismantled railway). Go over the bridge then between houses, following the access road through a small housing estate.

At a T-junction, leave the houses and go left into a light industrial estate, keeping to a pavement. This was the Old Town station when the railway line was in use! Just before the turning area at the end of the road, there is access, right, up steps into Newport Street. At a turning area, go right along an unsealed path past a mural, signed 'Wiltshire Cycleway'. Follow this, the Old Town railway line path, all the way back to the arch under the main railway behind Queensway and Texas, from there retracing your first few steps to the car park. At first, the railway path is in a cutting and under trees, but it soon opens out at the edge of the Old Town hill giving wide views across to the downs. Gradually dropping down as it heads west, the path passes just below the Princess Margaret Hospital (for the best views, climb up the intervening heathland slope and sit at the top on a sarsen stone), and crosses the disused Wilts and Berks canal before finally leaving the old railway embankment and passing round the edge of a field to reach the arch under the main railway.

The shorter, alternative route – The walk may be shortened quite easily at (*) by turning left, away from the footbridge over the motorway, and following the hedge on the left towards the farm. Pass to the right of the farm buildings, cross a bridge over a stream and take the concrete farm drive uphill to join the railway line path and follow it back to the start.

POINTS OF INTEREST:
The Old Town Railway Line – The path was built along the disused Swindon to Marlborough and Southampton line to provide a traffic-free route avoiding the busy streets of Old Town for pedestrians, cyclists, horse riders and wheelchairs. The funds were raised, and the work was carried out by groups of local volunteers, to provide access ramps and a smooth surface for wheels. Wiltshire County Council gave permission for the transformation and adopted the route as a public bridle path after its completion. The path links Southleaze and Mill Lane to Broome Manor, Coate Water and Burderop (and thence the downs). It now forms part of the long distance Wiltshire Cycleway route and is a highly valued amenity both to locals and to visitors.

The railway line path is also a haven for wildlife, providing plenty of shelter and an unfarmed habitat. Look out for rabbits, foxes, and badgers, both along the railway line and through the fields. Of the birds seen from the line perhaps the most spectacular is the occasional low-flying heron.
Sheep Milking Farm – The parlour, shop and farm are worth a visit even if refreshments are not required. Open in the afternoons from March to December (phone to check details) you can feed the ewes, see lambs, watch shearing and spinning and

browse in the shop where not only foods but also wool, crafts and gifts are sold. Clearly, no dogs are allowed.

REFRESHMENTS:
The sheep milking farm (tel no: 0793 523134). Try the delicious sheep's milk cheeses, yoghurts, fudge, ice cream and milkshakes.
Several pubs or shops along Newport Street before the final leg along the Old Town railway line path.

Walk 59 CLYFFE PYPARD AND BROADTOWN HILL 6m (9.5km)
Maps: OS Sheets Landranger 173; Pathfinder SU 07/17.
A walk along field paths and quiet lanes.
Start: At 074770, by the church in Clyffe Pypard village.

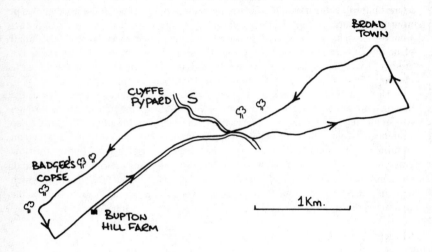

Enter the village churchyard and follow the stone set path to the right. This soon becomes a grassy track with an ornamental lake left. The church and manor house make a very pleasant scene, with the lake, all set below the overhanging branches of the beeches on the slopes above. Retrace your steps from the lake through the churchyard. Walk round to the north side and notice the private entrance from the manor to the church, with the Goddard crest on a stone plaque above the doorway. Leaving the churchyard, bear left through the village street, past the Goddard Arms to the crossroads. Bear right here and walk for about 100 yards, then take a lane on the left which bends up the hillside. Just past a farm on the left, go through the metal gate on the right. Follow this lane, which is metalled, down to another gate, pass through and follow the grassy track around the hillside. Always keep half-way up the hillside when following this path over several pole fences between the fields. When about opposite

122

a large farm in the plain below, watch carefully for a steep track ascending the downs at a point where there is a small new plantation on its right.

Take this path to a small metal gate. Pass through and turn sharp left. Follow the path around the edge of the field along the fence. When the fence ends head across the field towards a gap in the hedge. Turn right, and a few yards later emerge into a farm track. Turn left here and pass through Bupton Hill Farm. Go through the farmyard into a lane and follow the metalled road forwards for about 1 mile. A main road comes in from the left up a steep hill. Bear right here and go forward for about $^1/_4$ mile to a signpost. Take the lane to the left for Broad Hinton. Pass a small copse and then a small plantation of beech trees. In about $^1/_4$ mile the hedge on the left thickens and there is a group of five trees on the right. About 200 yards beyond, turn left into the fields at the opening. This left turn is just before the lane itself bends right.

Head straight across the field to reach a barbed wire fence on the edge of the downs. Turn left here and follow the path along the edge of the fields, passing through two small metal gates. (In some places this path is very muddy and needs care). Keep straight ahead along the edge of the downs. Do not take any paths off right. After about $^3/_4$ mile a track comes in from the right and merges with your path. Follow the now grassy track forward for about 400 yards, the last part along the right edge of a field. On gaining the road bear half-right and at the junction ahead take the road right which descends very steeply through thick beech woods into Clyffe Pypard. Follow the signpost right (marked 'Church') for the Goddard Arms and the start.

REFRESHMENTS
The Goddard Arms, Clyffe Pypard (tel no: 079373 386).

Walk 60   AROUND MILTON LILBOURNE $6\frac{1}{4}$m (10km)

Maps: OS Sheets Landranger 173 & 174; Pathfinder SU 06/16, 26/36, 05/15 & 25/35.

A walk on downland above the vale of Pewsey with superb views.

Start: The church, Milton Lilbourne.

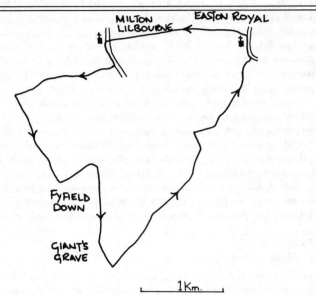

Walk on down the main street, past the Post Office, until you reach a track on the right, marked as a bridleway to Fyfield. Continue along this until it is joined by a track on the right and then runs along the edge of a large field. At the end of this field, turn left, following the line of the hedge towards the hillside beyond. You may just be able to make out the tiny shape of a white horse on the slope to the right. In the top right-hand corner of the field, pass through a small gate and follow the narrow path through trees. As the bushes to the left eventually peter out and the path runs along the edge of a field, head towards the black wooden barn and the windpump which are now visible. Continue along the path which leads straight on up the hillside, but half-way up bear left between abandoned gateposts (old railway sleepers) on a wide, chalky path. As you ascend, the views become increasingly spectacular, first the Vale of Pewsey on the left, then a great bowl-shaped valley on the right. The path runs in a horseshoe shape along the top of the bowl. As you reach the far side look to the right for the strip lynchets (remains of an ancient, terraced field system) close to the valley bottom. As you continue to walk along the edge of the bowl you will eventually see on your left a vast long barrow known as the **Giant's Grave**.

Pass just to the left of the barrow to a gate in the fence beyond. The Right of Way cuts straight across the field, bearing slightly right to a gate in the opposite fence. Turn left at the road and continue in the same direction past the farm and on down the long, gentle hill beyond. At the bottom of the hill the track bears slightly left and uphill. Continue along it to the next gateway on the right (more railway sleeper gateposts) and follow the track along the right-hand edge of the field. At the end of the field, turn left along the path between two fences, and continue downhill until you reach a made up track. Pass below electricity pylons and follow the track to the right. Turn left at the next junction, crossing a footbridge with white handrails, then walk past several pretty, thatched cottages to **Easton Royal Church**.

Take the gravel track to the left just beyond the church, then follow the overgrown path beside the churchyard. After crossing the stile beneath the lime tree, climb the next stile immediately to the left and cross the small electric fence near the left-hand hedge. From here, bear slightly right towards the large tree near the shed, where an overgrown stile gives access to the track beyond. Continue in the same direction along the track to the gate into the next field. Follow the fence on the left to the next stile, then continue on down the track for $^3/_4$ mile or so until you return to Milton Lilbourne.

POINTS OF INTEREST:
Giant's Grave – It is not hard to imagine how ancient burial mounds such as this one must have lent credence to myths concerning the existence of giants.
Easton Royal Church – The church was built by the Earl of Hertford towards the close of the 16th century and has been frequently restored and repaired. There are some slight traces of a priory of White Canons here which was disbanded during the Reformation.

REFRESHMENTS:
Several places in Milton Lilbourne and Easton Royal.

125

Walks 61 and 62 **BISHOPSTONE** 6¹/₂m (10.5km) and 3m (5km)
Maps: OS Sheets Landranger 174; Pathfinder SU 27/37 & 28/38.
Easy gradients and along obvious tracks with good, level footing.
Start: At 245837, in the village of Bishopstone. Patrons may park
at the True Heart public house.

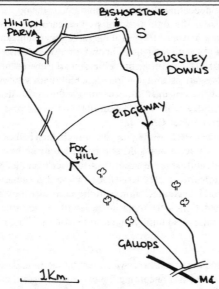

Leaving the True Heart, walk back the few yards to the main road and turn left along
it, then first right on to a narrow tarmac lane signed 'Russley Downs'. Almost
immediately, just past the house on the right, turn right on to a gravel drive, signed
'Public Footpath'. There is a view from here up the valley to the downs. At the end of
the drive pass between staddle stones, where the track becomes narrow and rather
muddy by a hedge. The route goes along the side of a small, narrow valley with a stream
at the bottom. Go through a wishing gate into a pasture field. Follow along the bottom
of a six-foot high bank on the left and leave the field at the far side by a wire-and-stake
gate to join a double earth track (may be muddy). Go left along the track. Look up the
valley to the right and see the **strip lynchets** at its head. The track now curves slightly
left into a sheltered, narrow valley, flat-bottomed with steep sides. The path runs along

126

the right edge. Go through a farm gate. The path, now bearing to the right continues up the valley. On the left are many small hillocks, to the right is a steep bank of valley side. The path now divides: one route going along the valley bottom, the other along the top right edge. They merge again as the valley opens out. At the far side of a field go through a hunting gate beside a farm gate and signpost, on to the Ridgeway (*). Cross it and continue along an obvious double earth track between arable fields. As the path gently rises, turn and enjoy the view behind, of plain beyond escarpment.

Pass by another track off to the left. A high point is reached with views all around. The grassy track continues and over the brow of the hill, now unfenced. Go through a farm gate, then follow the fence on the right. The track may be muddy here, but after another farm gate, by a barn on the right, is grassy once more, passing through a pasture field. Beyond the next farm gate, the route heads down a broad, shallow valley – the M4 motorway can be seen and heard ahead – crossing along a hillside. Pass through a gate into the last field, and leave it by a farm gate on to a narrow, tarmac lane. To the left here **Russley Park** can be seen.

Turn right up to a bridge over the motorway but go right just before it. Go through a hunting gate and keep right to follow a bridlepath with a fence on your right, *not* alongside the M4. The grassy double track between the fence and gallops now goes gently uphill. There are views in all directions – at 11 o'clock is Liddington Hill, and at 4 o'clock Lambourne Vale. The fence on the right ends temporarily leaving the track open. It may be muddy on this stretch. The gallops end but the route continues, the fence again being on the right. There is a radio mast ahead, on the top of Fox Hill. Heading for this the track briefly dips down before ascending again, through a hunting gate and between two fences, to the highest point of the walk – Fox Hill, 790ft. A dry, grassy track continues. Just beyond the brow, the tremendous views including Swindon at 11 o'clock (tallest feature: David Murray-John building). You will also, at the right time of year, notice a change in the **birdlife** over the last section of the route.

At the barn on the right, go through a hunting gate and cross the Ridgeway again (**). Continue straight on through a second hunting gate where the broad grassy track bends left downhill to a road, but keep to the fence on the right. Go straight on and through a hunting gate, downhill to a farm gate on to the road. Cross the road and continue straight on, signed 'Little Hinton', with a house on the left. The single track here may be muddy. Go through a hunting gate and into an area with numerous bark-chipping gallops. Keep straight on, crossing these as necessary and then walk between a scant double hedge (a single, possibly muddy track). Go through a farm gate and keep to the right along the top of a very narrow, steep-sided valley. There is an interesting view to left up the valley where strip lynchets can clearly be seen. The track gradually drops down the side of the valley into Hinton Parva (or Little Hinton). The track can be muddy at the lower end where there is a stream on the left of the field.

Go through a field gate by a house, on to a road. Go right along the road for 100 yards (keep on the left to avoid being hidden by the bend) then take the footpath on the left, signed 'Church'. Go through two wishing gates at either side of a paddock and into the picturesque village. Continue straight on at the tree in the triangle between roads, passing the church on the left. Where the lane bends sharp right, the footpath goes straight ahead between a cottage and some garages. Go past the graveyard and through a wishing gate. Continue on through two rather marshy fields via farm gates. Cross a stile on to a road. Follow the road for less than 1 mile into Bishopstone, keeping to the left-hand side until around the first right-hand bend. Pass Bishopstone village pond (dip your feet and/or dog as required) and return to the car and refreshments at the True Heart pub.

The shorter, alternative route – A very enjoyable walk of approximately half the length is easily achieved by linking the two marks (*) and (**). On reaching the Ridgeway go right along it until rejoining the main route at Fox Hill. The downs section of the route could be tackled by parking the car at the Shepherd's Rest pub, where the Ridgeway (see Walk 56) is crossed by the Ermin Way Roman road.

POINTS OF INTEREST:

Strip lynchets – These terraces are a typical feature of the downs here. From a distance they look rather like a giant staircase up the hillside. They are prehistoric, man-made, terraced fields created in order to farm crops on land which was otherwise too steep. Three or four thousand years ago they grew wheat and barley. Much later sheep farming became more profitable and the downs reverted to open grassland. Only when the Second World War prevented the grain ships getting through from the United States did the downs once again yield to the plough.

Russley Park – Close to the farthest point of the walk, not far from Baydon, will be of interest to those who follow horse racing. It was once a splendid race training establishment with 100 horses in training. Quite self-contained, it housed its own farrier and vet as well as grooms, gallops men, jockeys, trainers and house staff. Even gas lighting was provided by harvesting the methane produced from so much waste material! However, fighting with the British cavalry during the World War, the owner of the estate was deeply saddened by the terrible plight of the cavalry horses, and on his return he gave his entire stock – including that from his stud farm in Ireland – to the nation, thus founding the National Stud.

Birdlife – A bird of particular interest which may be heard in this area (around the villages rather than on the downs) is the Grasshopper Warbler. Its call is an unmistakable, prolonged metallic whirring or clicking sound. High on the downs your constant accompaniment will be the cheerful song of the skylark.

REFRESHMENTS:
The True Heart Inn, Bishopstone (tel no: 0793 790461). Accommodation is also available there.
The Shepherd's Rest, Liddington (tel no: 0793 790266).

Walk 63   **ANCIENT WILTSHIRE**   6¹/₂m (10.5km)

Maps: OS Sheets Landranger 173; Pathfinder SU 06/16 & 07/17.
The huge stone circle at Avebury and other important archaeological sites.
Start: The car park in the centre of Avebury.

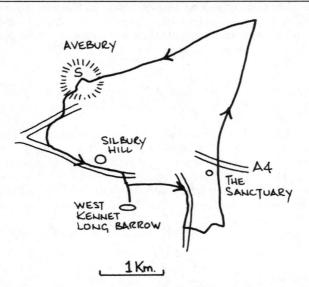

From the car park turn right for 50 yards, then left down a path. (To visit the museum and church, both very worthwhile, continue down the village street and turn right through the churchyard: then retrace steps.) Turn right in front of a sports field along a footpath. At the corner of a field, turn left through a gate and cross the field to a road. Turn right, then left after 100 yards along path signposted 'Silbury'. Turn right over a bridge and continue along the fenced path to a road. Turn left. After 300 yards turn left up a footpath to the summit of **Silbury Hill**. Descend by the same route and turn left.

Turn right through gate on marked path to **West Kennet Long Barrow**. (This sombre stone chambered tomb was built about 2,500 BC.) Retrace your steps for nearly ¹/₄ mile. Where the paths swings left, turn right through a gateway and follow the left-hand side of the field to a gate; go through and along a farm track. Cross the road and go through a gate. Follow a gated path on the right-hand side of the field to a gate at a crossing of tracks. Follow the track straight ahead. At a lane turn left and descend to East Kennet. At a T-junction turn right. After 100 yards, just after a road sign indicating the next T-junction, turn left along an alley beside a house. Turn left on to a road and follow the left fork to a bridge over the River Kennet. Cross river and ascend faint grass path along left-hand edge of field. Here is **The Sanctuary**.

Cross the road and walk along the wide grass path, the Ridgeway, for nearly 2 miles. At the crossing of paths, turn left following the sign 'Avebury $1^1/_2$'. Where the track becomes a lane, continue straight ahead through the **Avebury** stone circle and across the main road into the village and car park.

POINTS OF INTEREST:

Silbury Hill – The largest man-made mound in Europe, standing over 130 ft high and covering five acres. It was built, in four phases, about 4,500 years ago, but its use is a mystery.

West Kennet Long Barrow – An enormous neolithic burial chamber, over 100 yards long and with an entrance of huge sarsen stones.

The Sanctuary – Two circles of sarsen stones erected by Bronze Age people of Avebury, and marking a circular building, perhaps a temple. A 50ft wide avenue of standing stones once led, for more than 1 mile, from Avebury to the Sanctuary and many of these can still be seen along the roadside where the secondary road connects Avebury with West Kennet.

Avebury – The largest stone circle in Europe, a huge and impressive monument. One stone of the inner Great Circle weighs over 40 tons.

REFRESHMENTS:

The Red Lion, Avebury (tel no: 06723 266).

Walk 64   AROUND CROFTON   7m (11km)

Maps: OS Sheets Landranger 174; Pathfinder SU 26/36.

A basically level walk including woodland, open parkland and interesting canal features.

Start: At 235633, near the Savernake Hotel.

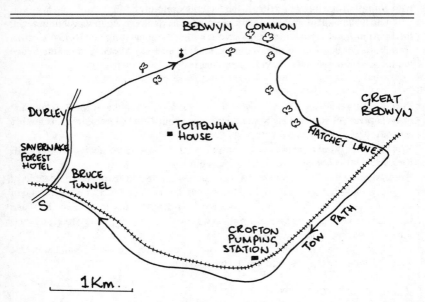

Set off along the metalled road to Durley looking out for a signpost on the right in $^1/_2$ mile to 'St Katharine's – $1^3/_4$ miles'. As an alternative to the road near the hotel, parking is also possible on a grassy verge by the signpost. Follow the line indicated, crossing a field towards a patch of woodland. Go through this woodland, over several stiles and an approach road to Tottenham House, to reach a large field. Make for the central of three clumps of trees and reach another stile on the far side of the field. The way now continues through woodland to reach **St Katharine's Church**.

Just beyond the church follow the signpost towards Stokke along the southern fringe of Bedwyn Common and passing a 'No Through Road' sign. At a junction of paths bear right up a rise and turn right again on reaching a large cottage. In 150 yards, bear left at a crossroads of pathways. On reaching a beautifully restored old house, bear right on to a much less well-defined path. Descend a little and then bear left at a parting of the ways. The track is now Hatchet Lane, running fairly straight in a depression between open fields, to reach the metalled road at the western edge of Great Bedwyn village (see Walk 36). Proceed straight forward, over the railway and the Kennet and Avon canal (see Walk 9), and immediately turn right to reach the towpath. Turn left and walk for just over 3 miles to return to the Savernake Hotel and start. Along the way you will note the abundant water fowl, the restored canal locks rising to the summit level, the Crofton pumping station (see Walk 38), the abutments of skew bridges which carried the Midland and South Western Junction Railway over the canal, the Bruce tunnel, with its plaque over the eastern portal. As there is no towpath through the tunnel, follow the track which angles up to the left just before the tunnel.

POINTS OF INTEREST:
St Katharine's Church – Designed by Wyatt and built in 1861 but now considerably altered. Notable churchyard with firs, cypresses and ha-ha.

REFRESHMENTS:
The Savernake Hotel (tel no: 0672 810206).

Walk 65   **PURTON AND RINGSBURY CAMP**   7¹/₂m (12km)
Maps: OS Sheets Landranger 173; Pathfinder SU 08/18.
A varied walk through pasture and woodland.
Start: At Purton Church, opposite the main entrance.

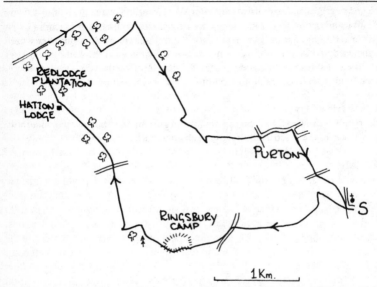

Walk away from **Purton Church** towards the T-junction, passing the beautiful manor house and barn. Cross the road and take the cycle track opposite, bearing left immediately. Cross the stile and bear right across the field towards the cluster of houses to the right of the school. Just after the stile in the opposite hedge, turn left on a path. As the field opens out to your right, bear right towards the stile in the middle of the opposite fence, cross this and bear right on a faint path across a field to the stile in the right-hand hedge. Keeping the hedge on your left, continue through several fields to reach a road. Turn left then at the next turning on the right, cross the road and take the grassy track to the left of the manor house tennis courts. After climbing a stile, turn left and follow the line of the hedge until you reach another stile near **Ringsbury Camp.** Turn left and shortly cross a stile on the right, following the outside of the fortifications all the way to the stile at the far end. Continue in the same direction across the field beyond, staying parallel with the left-hand hedge. The path is not easy to follow here: scramble down the bank beneath a large oak tree and press on until you see another stile ahead. The track beyond leads along the edge of the wood. At the bottom of the hill a field opens up to the right. Cross this through the gap in the hedge, right, and then follow the wide, grassy track until you reach a road. Cross the road and take the track opposite between two cottages and into the wood. After about $^3/_4$ mile you reach Hattons Lodge: look left for a view of the lake. Bear right at the drive of the house to a T-junction. Cross the field opposite and climb the gate on the other side. Follow a track through trees until you reach the edge of the wood. Turn right, following the path just inside the trees. After passing a five-barred gate, right, continue to the next track on the right. Follow this to a gate into fields, then turn left along the outside of the wood towards a stile in the next hedge. Now head for the visible gate ahead, keeping fairly close to the edge of the wood.

Once inside the copse, turn right and follow the track to a white gate. Continue in the same direction keeping the hedge on your right. Walk up the track past the farm, bearing right until you reach a gate. Go through and look for the first, low, double stile in the hedge to your left. Walk straight up the hill towards the large barn on the horizon and climb the stile to its left. Continue ahead into the field beyond, from which there are spectacular views of the surrounding countryside. Bear slightly right towards the far right-hand corner of the field and cross the next field keeping close to the hedge on your right. Climb the stile at the bottom and bear slightly left towards the furthest right of three large houses in the lane below you. Turn right at the road and almost immediately left along a stony track. Continue for about 400 yards until a break in the wooden fencing on your right allows you to reach a tiny alley between garden fences. Follow to a field and head up the hill towards the house with four small gables. Follow another small alley just to the right of this house, cross the road and continue up a flight of steps on the other side. At the school buildings turn left. At the chapel turn right. Take the first left fork and at the end of the cottages bear right along the path past the cemetery and back to the church.

POINTS OF INTEREST:
Purton Church – The church is slightly unusual in having both a tower and a spire. Inside are the remains of some frescoes and some old glass.
Ringsbury Camp – An impressive oval earthwork with a double ditch.

REFRESHMENTS:
The Angel Hotel, Purton (tel no: 0793 770248).
The Hope Inn, Purton (tel no: 0793 770482).

Walks 66 and 67   **LOCKERIDGE** $7^3/_4$m (12.5km)
Maps: OS Sheets Landranger 173; Pathfinder SU 06/16.
Part woodland, part downland – two sections easily split into two separate walks.
Start: At 147679, in the village of Lockeridge. Patrons may park at the Who'd A Thought It public house.

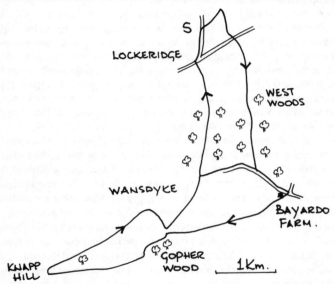

From the pub car park go left along the road. After the last house on the right, at a signpost for Fyfield, bear right through a farm gate and across a field along a visible path. Go over a stile and continue across the next field. Through a gateway, a double earth track leads between the River Kennet and a hedge. This may be muddy if wet. Go over a stile by a farm gate and follow the fence right to another stile, beyond which is the end of a tarmac lane. Go right along an earth track under trees (there is no Right of Way on a parallel hardcore track). The trees form a tunnel which the bridle path passes through! It will be muddy here if it is very wet, until a stony section is reached at the top end. The track comes out on to a road by a cottage. Go left along the road then, shortly, right along a hardcore track under trees. This becomes an earth and grass track.

Pass through a hunting gate and go straight on into West Woods. At a junction with a broader, vehicle-used track, go right. At a path crossroads, go on, steadily uphill. At the next junction of paths, again go straight on. Cross a narrow, unsealed road and continue on. The route now crosses the Wansdyke (see Walk 32), a low earth mound and ditch easily recognised by the corresponding break in the tree canopy. Further on the path broadens with vehicle use. Cross another broad track and continue straight on. As the route drops down to the visible edge of the woods, a long barrow, a neolithic burial chamber, can be seen among the trees to the right.

At the bottom of the slight slope, join a broad hardcore track and go left along it just within the edge of the wood (*). At the tarmac road by Bayardo Farm, go right up an unsealed road leaving the woods behind. At a barn on the left, go through a hunting gate just before the barn, rather than through the farmyard. Go round behind the barn and follow the hedge line right. Cross over a stile and turn right along the hedge. In a corner of the field, go through a hunting gate and along the path between fences (if overgrown here, go through the field just left of the path, rejoining it as soon as possible). Go past a barn on the right and over the brow of a very slight hill and **Gopher Wood** can be seen ahead with the sharp edge of the escarpment to the left.

At the bottom of the dip, go straight on through a hunting gate by a farm gate (**). Follow an obvious track across heathland climbing gradually around the edge of Gopher Wood. Go over a slot stile into a field and follow the fence, left, at the very edge of the wood. Cross a second slot stile, then go across a field to the left end of a line of trees at the edge of the escarpment by a signpost for **Knap Hill**. There are extensive views across the Vale of Pewsey from the route along the top of the escarpment.

Go right along the edge of the escarpment on a grass path by a line of stunted hawthorn trees. Go over a slot stile by a farm gate and straight on (reservoir tank on right) following the fence, right. The barely discernible summit of Golden Ball Hill is passed (879ft) before you begin descending. Go over a slot stile and straight on, still on the edge of the steep escarpment, before dropping down to a saddle between a spur of the ridge and Knap Hill.

To conquer Knap Hill go through a slot by a farm gate (information plaque on Pewsey Down National Nature Reserve, see Walk 32), cross the saddle and go up to the summit for the views from this Neolithic camp. Return through the farm gate. Go through a metal hunting gate in the fence at right-angles to the farm gate and go right, approximately following the fence line, right, away from the escarpment. In approximately 300 yards, go right through a break in the fence line, by some wire-fence sheep-pens and passing a water reservoir tank on the right. Keep along the fence on the right and head towards some groups of trees with a dew-pond. Go left in front of the trees, over a hunting jump in the fence and down a shallow valley keeping the fence/ hedge on the left. There is no obvious footpath here. You pass an old dew-pond on the other side of the arable valley and another track comes in from the right between double hedges. Go through a metal hunting gate and continue down the valley towards a mixed wood, with the fence now on the right. At the end of a pasture field, cross a hunting gate then carry on between a fence and a hedge. After another hunting gate, the track is overgrown in the dip, so go to the left of the hedge and bushes, still following the line of the track down through the field. Go through the hunting gate in the bottom of the valley, then along a broad double track slightly up again on the other side. Go through a farm gate under trees, then straight on across and down a field to a farm gate on the other side by some trees in the valley. Go through the gate, then left along a double earth track under trees (** joins from the right here).

Follow the narrow track down the valley. On re-entering the woods, cross the Wansdyke again (*** – keep a sharp look-out or you may miss it). Just into the woods and past the Wansdyke is a small muddy patch that is difficult to avoid. At the track beyond this go straight on, through a gateway (*not* uphill to right or left) and on down the valley on a broader, grassy path. At a large clearing in the woods, fork left along a slightly less obvious track which takes you out into the open across a clearing. Pass a picnic table on left and at the lowest point of the clearing cross a track at right-angles and then go on uphill. Go straight on to enter beech woods along an obvious, broad track. At an opening in the beech canopy, cross an unsealed road and continue on a broad avenue under trees. Leave the woods through a hunting gate near some farm buildings on the right. Keep the fence right and descend into a valley through a pasture field. At the far side, go through a hunting gate next to a farm gate and on down the slope between hedge and fence. At the bottom of the hill, go through a hunting gate on to a tarmac road at a junction. Take the road signed 'Marlborough' into Lockeridge village, passing a school and shop/Post Office on the left (use pavement on right). Return to the car park at the pub.

Shorter, alternative routes – This roughly figure of eight route is easily divided into two separate halves, a woodland walk and a downland walk. Simply connect the main walk directions of (**) where the route almost links but for about 10 yards. The woodland section would start from Lockeridge, the downland walk from the road across near Knap Hill. To stay entirely within West Woods simply turn right at (*) following the edge of the woods and then go along the Wansdyke to rejoin the main route at (***). This is a good option in the bluebell season.

The whole route, apart from the way off Golden Ball Hill, is along public bridle paths and may be enjoyed on horseback.

POINTS OF INTEREST:
Gopher Wood – Gopher, in Gopher Woods, refers to 'wrinkled' or 'wavy', not the small rodent!
Knap Hill – This 856ft hill was a Neolithic camp, with a commanding position overlooking the Vale of Pewsey. All this ancient landscape has a unique atmosphere through its obvious relics of past civilisations.

At the end of the walk, on returning to Lockeridge, visit Lockeridge Dene, a National Trust-owned field liberally sprinkled with sarsen stones or grey 'wethers' (they resemble sheep lying in the grass). Similar, but occupying a hidden valley North of the A4, is Pigheldene, another National Trust reserve. Sarsen stone was the building material of megalithic man – dense, heavy and impervious to water, it was formed when silica permeated the sandstone, leaving strange holes where the roots of palm trees once penetrated. Areas of sarsen stone occur naturally all over the downs.

REFRESHMENTS:
The Who'd A Thought It , Lockeridge (tel no: 067286 255).
Refreshments are also available from the shop in Lockeridge (picnic food, sweets, drinks etc).

Walks 68, 69 and 70   **HACKPEN HILL**   8m (13km), 3m (5km), 6¼m (10km)

Maps: OS Sheets Landranger 173; Pathfinder SU 07/17.

Easy and mostly level walking along obvious tracks.

Start: At 129747, where the Marlborough/Wootton Bassett road crosses the Ridgeway at Hackpen Hill.

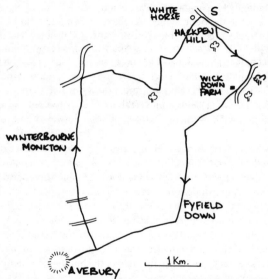

Set off left from the car park, along the road towards Marlborough going south-east and keeping to the grass verge. Please be careful, remembering to watch out for traffic. In about 350 yards turn right down an unsealed track, quite steeply downhill initially, then levelling out. There are some fine views from here. Where the track meets a tarmac lane at a T-junction, turn right along the tarmac lane and go over a slight rise. Pass through the yard of Wickdown Farm between the house and the out-buildings. Just beyond the yard, take a double earth track up to the brow of the hill, passing just to the right of a small clump of trees. Follow this track to a hunting gate by a cattle grid. Go through the gate and on to where the track is joined by another coming up from the valley on the left. This is grazing pasture, so please keep dogs under control.

At the far side of the field go through another hunting gate to reach a good place for a short stop, in the shelter of some stunted trees and bushes by two dew-ponds. No more climbing for now – enjoy the views behind you. Continue straight ahead from the hunting gate, beyond some bushes, to a farm gate opening on to the Ridgeway Long Distance Footpath. Turn left along the Ridgeway (see Walk 56), passing Fyfield Down Nature Reserve (see Walk 51) and some training gallops on the left (or detour along the Right of Way through the Reserve to rejoin the Ridgeway in 600 yards, adding an extra 400 yards to the walk).

Now as you gradually lose height, there are extensive views to the right. Take the obvious, broad track off to the right, signed 'Avebury', leaving Fyfield Down Nature Reserve behind. The track drops down more quickly now and then levels out. Ignoring the first Right of Way off to the right, continue down to some farm buildings and the next Right of Way will be found on the right after the first group of buildings, signed 'Winterbourne Monkton'.

(At this point you may wish to continue along the track, past the farm buildings, where the track becomes tarmac, and on into Avebury to visit the famous stone circles – a further 10 minutes' walk – where a rest stop can be enjoyed and refreshment obtained.)

The track to Winterbourne Monkton is broad and grassy with a fence on the right and passes through several gates. A tarmac track is crossed but you continue straight on and over the brow of a gentle rise. Dropping down again to some farm buildings, join a tarmac lane, still going straight on, between hawthorn hedges. At a T-junction in the tarmac lanes, go straight over on to a broad grassy track with a hedge on the left. The route now joins a double earth track skirting to the right of some farm buildings. Continue ahead: a windpump should be visible ahead half-left. At a track crossroads (with a double-hedged track to the right) go straight on towards a farm building. The route here is an unfenced track, passing to the right of the building. From this point the track can be very muddy in wet weather.

Just as the track meets the A361, the road bends sharply to your left and the route turns to your right along an unsealed lane, signed 'Ridgeway'. Pass to the right of the farm buildings (another section that can be muddy) then continue between a double hedge, heading back towards the Downs. Berwick Bassett Clump is the rather grand name of the meagre stand of trees on the skyline. The double hedge ends at a farm gate where the track enters a pasture field just below the hill. Follow the track around to the right of the hill, climbing until a fence corner can be seen to the left, before the gate is reached. Go to the fence corner and, with the fence on the right, follow it along the top of a steep field, with a clump of trees beyond the fence. Go through the gate at the end of the field, then go right along a double earth track for a short distance to join the Ridgeway at the next gateway. Go left along the Ridgeway and follow its broad track all the way back to the car parking at **Hackpen Hill**.

Shorter, alternative routes – Two alternative, shorter walks are simply arranged by walking either loop of this almost figure of eight route separately:

A.   When reaching the dew-ponds on the ridge after Wickdown Farm, turn right between the ponds and join the Ridgeway after a gate under trees, then go straight ahead back to the car (total 3 miles or 5km).

B.   From the car, walk south along the Ridgeway and join the main route as it approaches Fyfield Down Nature Reserve (total $6^1/_4$ miles or 10km).

The linking section of the Ridgeway, one of Europe's oldest roads – some 90 miles of its still existing length has been made into a Countryside Commission Official Long Distance Path, running from Ivinghoe Beacon in the east to Overton Hill (near Avebury) in the west – also serves as an emergency escape route in case of illness or deteriorating weather.

There are no stiles to be climbed along any of this route, all access being through hunting or farm gates.

POINTS OF INTEREST:
Hackpen Hill – The hill's name derives from the Old English, *Laca pen*, hook hill. On its northern flank there is a white horse cut in 1838 to celebrate the Coronation of Queen Victoria. The horse measures 90ft by 90ft.

Magnificent views can be enjoyed from almost any point along this walk – don't forget an occasional glance behind, too. The endlessly rolling chalk downs almost give the sensation of being far out to sea. Throughout the walk you will hear the song of the skylark, and if you are lucky (and sharp-eyed) you may see a short-eared owl, a daytime hunter.

REFRESHMENTS:
There are a number of possibilities at Avebury, but no other refreshments anywhere

else on this route. If you do not plan to visit Avebury it would be wise to carry your own food and/or drink, especially in extremes of weather.

In Avebury try:

The Red Lion (tel no: 06723 266).

Stones Restaurant (tel no: 06723 514).

Avebury Manor (tel no: 06723 203).

There is also a small Post Office and general store.

Walk 71 ALL CANNINGS AND STANTON ST BERNARD 8m (13km)

Maps: OS Sheets Landranger 173; Pathfinder SU 06/16.

A walk on open downland.

Start: At 073620, the triangular road junction in All Cannings.

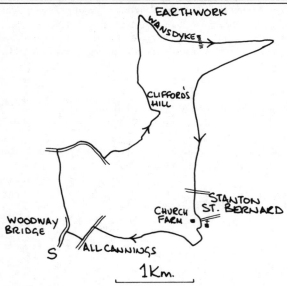

Follow the cul-de-sac road towards Townend. At the edge of the village fork left ('Byway to Woodway Bridge'). Cross the Kennet and Avon canal at the bridge and proceed to the Devizes-Pewsey road along a lane which may be muddy in wet weather. Turn right at the road, which is not usually very busy, and take the broad trackway to the left opposite Cannings Cross farm (after about 600 yards). Take the right fork, marked footpath, at a stile and climb steeply up the end of Cliffords Hill. Follow the broad grassy ridge until the path bends to the left and descends slightly before rising to **Rybury Camp**.

After exploring the earthworks drop to a farm gate and join a well-marked path, bearing right, and going gradually uphill. This path passes close to a hill summit at 294m before joining the ancient Wansdyke (see Walk 21). Turn right and follow the dyke for nearly $1^1/_2$ miles. There are now fine views to the north, views which include Silbury Hill. At an unmade roadway turn sharp right. There is now a choice between a path and a road, each descending towards Stanton St Bernard. Above and to the left is a slope much favoured by hang gliders at weekends. Just after passing the drive to Hill Barn take the left fork, carry straight on at the next farm building and cross the Devizes-Pewsey road, heading for **Stanton St Bernard**.

Go straight ahead, then right at Church Farm, passing the Pewsey Vale riding centre, then left on to a broad trackway leading to the Kennet and Avon canal. Turn left along the towpath until the All Cannings road is reached. Turn left on this road and, in 100 yards, turn right at a by-way sign, along the edge of a field, to reach **All Cannings** and the start.

POINTS OF INTEREST:
Rybury Camp – Iron Age hill fort with prominent ditch and banking.
Stanton St Bernard – Rather isolated village. The church, with the exception of the perpendicular tower, dates from 1833.
All Cannings – Some good thatched houses. Sizeable church – Norman, Early English, Perpendicular, Victorian. Post Office/general stores.

REFRESHMENTS:
The Kings Arms, All Cannings (tel no: 038086 328).

Walks 72 and 73   **BARBURY CASTLE**   9m (14.5km)

Maps: OS Sheets Landranger 173; Pathfinder SU 07/17.

An open downland walk, visiting two old picturesque villages.
Mostly along obvious paths with good level footing.

Start: At 156760, the large car park at Barbury Castle.

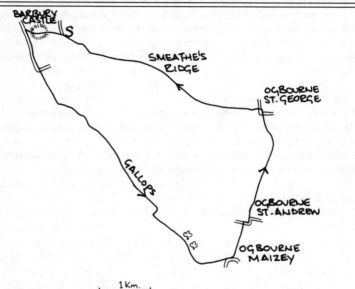

After looking at the extensive views over Swindon and beyond, walk to **Barbury Castle** itself, an Iron Age hill fort earthworks (but do not expect stone ramparts!). From the hunting gate beyond the public conveniences and information display, cross the level field (pasture) and go through another hunting gate. Either walk through the centre of the fort or along the top of the perimeter earth walls. Beyond the hill fort go through the next hunting gate and down a fairly steep track to a last hunting gate on to a tarmac road (there is an information plaque and signpost here). Turn left along a narrow road, going gently downhill. From here there are fine views ahead across downs. Where the tarmac ends (and Barbury Castle Farm's private road goes off to the left) follow a double track straight on, down a slight dip and then up again. Pass through a gateway and the U-bend of some training gallops can be seen just ahead. Join the edge of the gallops and go left. Go gently downhill and follow the gallops around to the right where a double grass and chalk track branches off along the left side of the gallops. It will possibly be muddy in places here. Note the ancient field system on slope to left. The track curves around small spurs and valleys, following the contours. On reaching the corner of a fence on the left, go through a farm gate into a pasture field on the side of the escarpment and keep along the fence on the right. The path gradually rises and on rounding a spur of the hill can be seen bearing left and diagonally up the Ogbourne Maizey escarpment as a grassy path defined as a terrace in the slope of the hill. As you climb gradually, the road in the valley becomes visible away to right beyond the gallops. Below the escarpment is an ancient field system. At the top of the escarpment join a fence line on the left into a corner of a field by a shallow, circular depression (the remains of an old dew-pond). Climb a fence by a corner straining post (*the erection of a stile in this fence is being actively pursued by Wiltshire County Council, and should be in place by the end of 1989*) and go straight on to an obvious grassy track almost immediately. Go right, with fence to the right, until a track joins the gallops.

Cross straight over the gallops and on the far side cross a stony double track (*). Another track ahead leads to a modern barn on the skyline (fence on your left). Go past the barn and on reaching the upper end of the gallops – at a hedge – go right along the hedge. Where the hedge turns left, join a double stony track and follow it on the left with gallops on other side. Go slightly downhill, passing barns on the right, to where the gallops curve away left. Here the track continues down, beneath a hangar of mature beech trees, left, all the way into Ogbourne Maizey. At the road go straight along it for 50 yards then take a footpath on the left through a wishing gate, signposted 'Ogbourne St George'. (Dogs may find a welcome drink at the River Og just 50 yards beyond the footpath turn-off. Any further upstream is likely to be dry in summer.)

The footpath passes through a line of trees. Go over a stile into a field. Go over a stile on the far side, and straight on towards the church tower. Go across a farm track (or right along it and into the village of Ogbourne St Andrew to find the Wheatsheaf Inn and the village shop). From the farm track, pass between houses and gardens then go under a wooden archway into the churchyard. On the far side go through a gate on to a road and go right. At a T-junction go left for a short way until the road bends right and there take a double track to the left. Soon this divides: bear left again. A track passes between hedges, crosses a farm track and continues straight on. Where another track goes to the right, keep straight on (both directions are signed 'Ridgeway') passing between, then under, a hedge of trees. Go downhill to a road. Go straight ahead, following the signpost to the Ridgeway . About 50 yards along the road go left on to a broad concrete, then unsealed track, going slightly uphill and signed 'Ridgeway'.

At the brow of the hill, on a slight right bend, bear left over a stile by a farm gate, following a signpost for Smeathe's Ridge (**not** to right on the track between hedges). You go very gradually uphill all the way to **Barbury Castle** car park, following a well-defined grassy track. Go through a pasture using a stile and two gates. After the last gate an unfenced path runs across arable fields on the top of the ridge. Note the ancient field systems to the right. Finally go through a hunting gate on to a broad stony track (******) and go right, passing Upper Herdswick farm on right, into the car park.

Shorter, alternative routes – To divide the walk into two shorter loops (or for a quick return to the car park in any emergency) simply use the broad, stony track between (*****) and (******) in the main route directions, a stretch of 2 miles (3km).

POINTS OF INTEREST:
Barbury Castle is a recognised Country Park, with car park, picnic tables, public conveniences, information plaques, an ice cream van and marvellous views north. There is frequently hang gliding or kite flying to watch. The highest point of the walk is here, at 879ft (268m).

It was a very different place in the Iron Age. The hill fort, with its three clearly defined circles of ditch and mound, was a refuge for the people and their livestock who came from small settlements around in times of danger.

Barbury Castle and Smeathe's Ridge form part of the Ridgeway Long Distance Path, stretching from Ivinghoe Beacon in the east to Overton Hill on the A4 to the west. For most of the way the Long Distance Path follows the route of the ancient Ridgeway, probably the oldest road in Europe and certainly older than the Iron Age earthworks along it. The section of the path included in this walk is a modern deviation to avoid 4 miles of tarmac near Chiseldon (the ancient route passes below Barbury Castle on the very edge of the escarpment, thence towards Chiseldon and on to Fox Hill).

REFRESHMENTS:
Apart from the ice cream van at Barbury Castle on summer Sundays and bank holidays, try:
The Wheatsheaf Inn, Ogbourne St Andrew (tel no: 067284 229).
The Robin Hood, Ogbourne St George (tel no: 067284 445). This is a little way off the route.
Both villages also have a general store.

Owing to the exposed nature of the majority of this route it is advisable to carry drinking water in hot weather (including some for dogs, as there are virtually no streams or troughs) and some food in cold weather.

Maps: OS Sheets Landranger 174; Pathfinder SU 27/37.
High downland with extensive views over the rolling country side.
Start: At 264756, in the centre of Aldbourne by the pond.

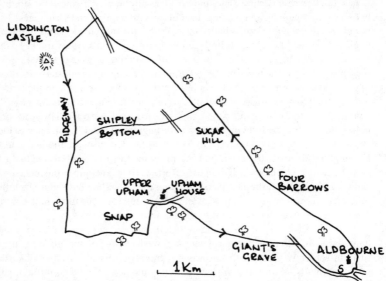

With the pond directly behind you, take the street north towards the church, passing the village green and the Blue Boar pub. Take the road to the right of the church, going slightly uphill. There are houses to the right near the bend at 'Crooked Corner'. About 100 yards further on take the obvious, broad, hardcore track forking left off the road, signed 'Public Right of Way', which goes slightly uphill under trees. The track becomes grassy, rising gradually and leaving trees behind to give views all around. The route reaches the brow of a hill beyond which it undulates gently. Pass through a farm gate beyond which the still-broad grassy track winds between the first and second of four Neolithic burial mounds – the Four Barrows.

　　Pass a small wood on right, after which the M4 can be seen (and faintly heard) away to the right across the side of the hill. The route climbs gently, but barely noticeably to the brow of Sugar Hill, with a wood on the right with extensive views in all other directions.

Go down a brief drop to a junction with a track coming in from the right where the woods end. Go left and through a farm gate. (There is an escape route to the road here – go straight ahead downhill for 600 yards.) Go right immediately after the gate and through another farm gate, then go left to follow the fence line off left along a broad, grassy track across pasture. The route is clear all the way, rising very slightly again before dropping down and passing through several hunting and farm gates. There is a muddy section where farm vehicles pass. Where the farm track bends to the right, go straight on through a gate and climb gently uphill again on a grassy track. To the right, you can see the mast on the top of Fox Hill. Beyond the next gate, the track is less obvious, so keep to the fence on the left ultimately going alongside the road, but staying in the field. Just before the road reaches a crossroads, cross a stile in the fence on the left by a signpost. Cross the road with care, the traffic can be a little fast here, and go straight ahead through a gate by the signpost on to a hardcore track. This leads gradually uphill, but climbing a little more steeply, through farm gates. Look back to the left to see a view of the route you have followed so far. Go through another gate (*) and Liddington Castle can be seen ahead. At this point, the path bends round to the left. To visit the castle, which is worth the extra effort, go right, keeping to the fence line on the right. Go through a farm gate then left along the fence line until you reach the earth ramparts of this excellent example of an Iron Age hill fort. The fort is half-way and also the highest point on the walk. From it, the views are superb.

If you have visited the castle, return to the gate at (*) and continue along the hardcore path. After the next farm gate, follow the hedge on the left along the flat top of the hill on a now grassy path. Go through a muddy farm gateway after which the route drops gradually down through pasture. When the hedge ends, go through gates and follow the track, which is now not always obvious, through fields. Keep to the fence on your left. Go through a hunting gate beyond which the path runs between fences. Another track comes in from the left (you can go down this for another escape route to the road). Pass trees on the left and then a possibly muddy patch. At a T-junction of tracks, go right then almost immediately left, to continue in the same direction as before. There are fine views to the right when the track passes under trees.

At an obvious crossroads of tracks, by water tanks and with a mast clearly seen off to right, go left along a hardcore track. After about 300 yards, the track forms a right-angle to the right. Our route goes straight on, over a stile, and down a small, narrow valley along vehicle tracks and across pasture. At a corner of the fence line on the right, where the tracks bend left to go on down the valley, keep straight on, going along the fence. In 40 yards, you will reach an inwards corner of the fence. Here, go straight on through a gateway and into a wood. This was the site of **Snap** village, deliberately abandoned in the last century to make more room for sheep.

Another track comes in almost immediately from the right under the trees. Continue on along the double, grassy path between two fences, passing a signpost for a footpath off to the right. It may be muddy under the trees. Go left and slightly downhill, crossing the valley, then right to follow the fence on the right. At a clear crossroads of tracks, go left along the hardcore double track, quite steeply uphill under trees. The track ends at a tarmac road for Upper Upham. Go right along the road. After a short distance, look left for a view of Upham House, a beautiful Tudor mansion built in 1599.

Where the road bends left, go through a farm gate on the right by a signpost, and along a broad, grassy path between fences. Go through another gate and then straight on across an open field to the next gate with a copse of trees beyond. The broad, double grassy track passes over the brow of a slight rise with the copse on the left. Go through open fields with views ahead. Dropping down the spur of the hill, pass through a farm gate with tumuli to the left. Go through a hunting gate and past a wood on the left. Another tumulus, Giant's Grave, is to the left of the path here. Go through a gate by a barn. At the main road, go right and keep on the right-hand side of the road to face oncoming traffic. Take care, this is a fast road. Carry on into the village and back to the car park and starting point.

Shorter, alternative routes – By linking up the two escape routes mentioned in the walk directions, known as Shipley Bottom or Sugar Way, the walk may be cut into two. Or, with two cars, one left at Aldbourne and the other at the 'dead leg' of the Ridgeway near Liddington Castle, either half of the walk could be tackled on its own. The B4192 Swindon/Aldbourne road bisects the route.

POINTS OF INTEREST:

Snap – Little remains of the village now, only heaps of stones among the trees. The few inhabitants were dispossessed when it was deemed that sheep were more profitable. A typical wage for those who lived there would have been about seven shillings (35p) a week. The name Snap suggests it was once a Viking settlement, dating from about the 11th century, but it does not figure in the Oxford Dictionary of English Place-Names because it had already ceased to exist when the dictionary was first published in 1936.

The route from Liddington Castle to the turn-off for Snap is along the Ridgeway Long Distance Path which stretches from Ivinghoe Beacon in the east to Avebury in the west. However, the ancient route of the Ridgeway passes to the north of Liddington Castle and on directly west. This diversion was created by the Countryside Commission to cut out nearly 4 miles of tarmac along the true Ridgeway, and in doing so added in some of the most beautiful stretches of the Marlborough Downs.

REFRESHMENTS:
Unless you carry your own food and drinks, the only opportunity for any refreshments is either before or after the walk, at Aldbourne. There are a number of pubs in the village and two small village shops.
The Blue Boar (tel no: 0672 40237) is very old, small and quaint.

Walks 76 and 77   **CHISELDON** $10^{1/_2}$m (17km)
Maps: OS Sheets Landranger 173 & 174; Pathfinder SU 07/17 & 27/37.

Easy walking with mostly level ground and gentle gradients.
Start: At 184794, the Patriots Arms, Chiseldon.

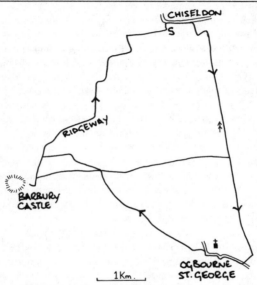

From the front of the pub, go right (east) using pavements, a footpath and wide grassy verges, to avoid the traffic. Just past Canney Close, a cul-de-sac on the left, a footpath is well signposted to the right at the edge of a field, following the hedge on the left. At the far end of the field, go over a stile into a lane. Go left along the lane for 200 yards. Before the main road (A435), turn right on to a disused railway line. This is the **Chiseldon to Marlborough Railway Line Path**.

Head south along the railway line.The main road is about 50 yards to the left running almost parallel to the path. After almost 1 mile, the path bends left off the railway line to pass between an embankment and the road, skirting a permanent gipsy camp and going through a clump of Scots Pines on to a tarmac lane. Go right then left to rejoin the railway line. The route passes between a double hedge of shrubs and trees, a real wildlife haven. Where a bridge once took the railway over a track at right-angles, but is now dismantled, the path descends to the track, on the left of the old bridge, crosses the track (*) and goes up the other side to rejoin the railway. Pass through a very sheltered cutting. Cross a tarmac lane, passing houses on the left with a farm down the lane to the right. Where the railway used to cross a track via a low bridge (now gone), descend to the right on to the track and go along it for 20 yards before doubling back to rejoin the railway line by some kennels.

A little further on, almost into Ogbourne St George, go up out of the cutting and go over a stile on to a concrete track at right-angles to the railway, towards some houses. This metalled lane is Jubb's Lane. A short way on into the village, at a T-junction, turn right. Follow the road through the village, past a school on the left, to pass a drive to the church on the right (worth a visit if time permits). Where the road goes right, and Ridgeway Long Distance Path is signposted left and right, go right with road for about 50 yards then left (signed for the Ridgeway) on to a broad concrete then unsealed track going slightly uphill. At the brow of the hill and a slight right bend, keep right on a grassy track (***not*** through the gate signed for Smeathes Ridge).

At first, the path runs between a double hedge, then between a double fence with pasture on the left, up the escarpment to the downs. This section is quite exposed so beware of extremes in the weather. When the fence on the right ends, you join a concrete farm road coming in from the right and continue straight on, past a conifer plantation and pens on the left. There is an earth track from herewith trees forming a hedge on the left. This section can be very muddy but the worst is avoidable.

After $1/2$ mile a double hedged track comes in from the right (**). Go left along a path signed for Burderop Down. There is a brief section under bushes/trees which can be muddy, but then you are out into the open. There is a signpost where the track divides. Bear left and uphill to Barbury Castle (see Walk 72) or to avoid the hill, bear right and along the track more or less straight on to rejoin the road below the castle. This grassy track with right and left dog-legs and then a section left along an unsealed farm road is easy to follow. On the castle route, there is a steep but brief climb to a stile by a wire-and-stake gate, then a more gradual climb, keeping the fence on the left. At the top, pause for breath and to take in the wonderful views. Looking north, with your back to the fence, you have at 11 o'clock – Wroughton airfield, 12 o'clock – Swindon partially hidden by the escarpment, 1 o'clock – Chiseldon, 2 o'clock – Liddington Hill and finally at 4 o'clock – Ogbourne St George. Go over a stile by a farm gate on to a road and go left for 50 yards to reach the Barbury Castle car park, the highest point of the walk at 880ft, where there are further panoramic views.

Retrace your steps to the road, go over a stile, through a farm gate and down the hill. (The route from the earlier option to miss out the steep climb joins the road from the right here.) After 300 yards, pass a track to the left, signed 'Ridgeway, Barbury Castle', and almost immediately take a track on the right along a section of the original Ridgeway. The track is very broad with numerous wheel ruts. It can also be very muddy but the worst is avoidable. Where the tracks go off left to a barn, the route becomes more grassy. Where the Ridgeway forms a left/right dog-leg, go around the left bend but then keep straight ahead, leaving the Ridgeway. Follow a sparse hedge on the left until at a gateway you draw level with a barn 100 yards to the left. A hardcore track comes towards you and turns at right-angles towards the barn. Turn right here, away from the barn, keeping at the edge of a field with a low hedge on the right. The hedge goes left, then right. Follow it round and now with a sparse hedge/fence still on your right, go into the next corner of the field. Pass through a gap in the fence to a T-junction with a bridle path. Go left, following the hedge on the left, until you see a well-formed single path running right, unfenced, across the last field into Chiseldon. Pass behind the first few houses and between the last gardens on to the Draycot road. Go left for 50 yards and the Patriots Arms car park is on the right.

Shorter, alternative route – A short cut to avoid the steepish climb to Barbury Castle is already included. A shorter walk, omitting Ogbourne St George and crossing the Lower Chalk between Chiseldon and Barbury Castle, is easily adapted from the main route. At (*) where the path descends from the railway line to a track at right-angles, instead of crossing the track and continuing along the railway route, go right along the track. Cross a road and continue straight on along the double-hedged track, which may be muddy, until a junction of tracks (**) is reached. Now continue as for the main walk, either to Barbury Castle or avoiding the hill. This alternative is 7 miles (11km).

POINTS OF INTEREST:
Chiseldon to Marlborough Railway Line Path – This was created by local volunteer workers, supported by the Local Authorities, from a long disused section of the line which once linked Swindon and Marlborough. It provides enjoyable, safe, easy walking or riding (the path is also for cyclists and horse riders) and a haven for wildlife in otherwise open, heavily cultivated farm land. Look out for a wide variety of wild flowers, insects, birds and animals. They will be protected for at least the 25 year lease period of the railway path – and hopefully for ever.

REFRESHMENTS:

This walk conveniently divides into three sections with refreshment opportunities after each.

The Robin Hood Inn, Ogbourne St George (tel no: 067284 445) is only a little way off route.

At Barbury Castle on summer Sundays and bank holidays there will almost certainly be an ice cream van.

The Patriots Arms, Chiseldon (tel no: 0793 740331).

Both Chiseldon and Ogbourne St George also have a Post Office and general store.

Walk 78   PEWSEY WHARF TO KNAP HILL   10¹/₂m (17km)

Maps: OS Sheets Landranger 173; Pathfinder SU 06/16.

Canal and downland combine to provide a substantial walk.

Start: Pewsey Wharf has space for parking several cars.

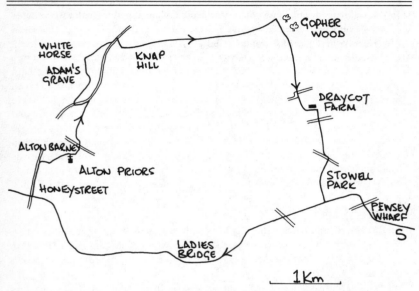

Proceed along the canal towpath towards Devizes, passing Stowell Park, a small suspension bridge and a swing bridge. In about 2 miles Ladies Bridge is reached. Here the canal looks like an ornamental lake as it passes through the grounds of Wilcot Manor. It is believed that Lady Wroughton would agree to sell land to the canal company only if it was constructed in this manner. This belief remains unproven! Continue to Honeystreet, with splendid views of Pickled Hill and Woodborough Hill. At Honeystreet leave the canal and follow the metalled road to **Alton Barnes**. Do not fail to divert for a short distance further along the towpath to the Barge Inn, a genuine canal-side pub, where refreshment of all kinds is available.

    Turn right in Alton Barnes following the sign 'Saxon Church'. Just before reaching the church pass through a revolving turnstile on the left and take the unusual cobbled path towards **Alton Priors** church. Go over two small bridges and through three more revolving stiles to reach the metalled lane in Alton Priors. Follow this lane to the Devizes-Pewsey road. Turn left, then almost immediately right into a minor road – from which the Ridgeway (see Walk 56) branches off to the right, climbing between trees towards the crest of the Downs. On reaching a metalled road, turn left and proceed downhill for 300 yards, then turn sharply right on to a well-defined chalky path, rising steeply from the road. The Pewsey Downs National Nature Reserve is shortly entered and a good path passes close to the long barrow known as Adam's Grave. The **Alton White Horse** is an optional diversion to the left. The views over the Pewsey Vale are extensive.

Follow the path which angles back to the metalled road, joining it at a stile. Turn left for a short distance and then right on to a wide track known as Workway Drove. Look out for a stile up a banking to the left shortly after passing through a gate. Make for another gate and notice board below the crest of Knap Hill. Go over the hill and continue along the edge of the Downs for a further mile. Just before reaching Gopher Wood turn sharp right and descend steeply by a well-used track to reach a metalled road a little to the north of Draycot Farm. Proceed past the farm, straight across a crossroads and, at a staggered junction bear right, following a 'Wilcot' posting, until the canal is reached. Turn left along the towpath to return to Pewsey Wharf in just under 1 mile.

POINTS OF INTEREST:

Alton Barnes, Alton Priors – Small hamlets with churches remarkably close together. St Mary's, Alton Barnes, shows evidence of its Saxon origins and has a Georgian gallery. Alton Priors church is old and simple and has escaped major Victorian restoration.

Alton White Horse – Cut in 1812 at the expense of Robert Pile, a local farmer. It is about 1,675 ft long and 160 ft high.

REFRESHMENTS:

The French Horn Inn near Pewsey Wharf (tel no: 0672 62443).
The Barge Inn, Honeystreet (tel no: 067285 238).

Walk 79   **SHERRINGTON AND BOYTON DOWN**   4m (6.5km)
Maps: OS Sheets Landranger 184; Pathfinder ST 83/93.
Fields, paths and a woodland track to reach one of the highest
points on the southern downlands.
Start: Sherrington Church.

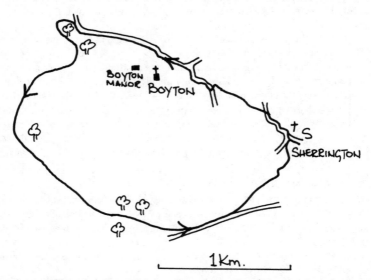

With **Sherrington Church** on your right, walk up the road to the point where it bears
left by **Rectory Cottage**. Take a rough track ahead of you and follow this until you
reach a metal gate on the left. Go through, turn immediately right and follow the field
boundary round until you reach a broken wooden fence with the remains of a stile.
Cross over into the next field and continue to follow the boundary hedge until an open
gate is reached which leads directly on to a metalled road. Here turn right and follow
the road down and round the bends. Ignore the signposted road on your right opposite
the main entrance to Boyton Manor and continue ahead. If you wish to visit Boyton
Church and Manor (the church is kept locked), turn left by a house with a postbox let
into its wall. Otherwise continue to follow the road until you eventually reach a
signposted turning right to Upton Lovell. Directly opposite this turning there is a track

160

leading left. Take this track which climbs up through trees from the valley bottom some 300ft (92m) to the top of Codford Hill.

Shortly after the track levels out you will pass farm buildings on your left and just beyond these the track emerges on to a metalled road. Turn left. You will soon pass three derelict farm cottages on your left and, further on, a clutter of farm machinery parked on the broad grass verge. Shortly after this point are two large cow barns and then to your left, you pass an ancient burial mound just beyond a gate on the left. A little further on from this tumulus the metalled road bears right and a rough track goes off to the left. Take this descending track and about $\frac{1}{4}$ mile further on look for a section of fence strengthened with a wooden frame to form a crossing place. Cross over into the field and go over a similar crossing in the fence directly opposite. Descend the cuesta to the boundary fence. Turn right and follow the fence until a metal gate is reached. Go through the gate and bearing slightly left walk to another metal gate. Go through this, cross the metalled road and then pass through a further metal gate opposite. Cross the field, bearing slightly left towards a stile. Cross the stile and then go over **Sherrington Mere** on a bridge made of old railway sleepers. On reaching the road, turn right and walk down to a junction by two thatched cottages. Here you can either turn left and walk the short distance to Rectory Cottage and the start, or continue to skirt the mere until a T-junction is reached. Turn left there and follow the road down to the church and start.

POINTS OF INTEREST:
Sherrington Church – Has an unusual dedication to two Middle Eastern Saints, Damien and Cosmos. A fine little medieval church well worth a visit.
Rectory Cottage – Note the Bible texts affixed to the end wall.
Sherrington Mere – Here watercress was grown commercially until Common Market regulations declared it unfit for such a purpose.

REFRESHMENTS:
Served in Sherrington.

Walk 80   AROUND TOLLARD ROYAL   4¹/₂m (7.5km)

Maps: OS Sheets Landranger 184; Pathfinder ST 81/91 & 82/92.
Well-marked tracks and commands some superb views. One short, steep scramble.
Start: At 944178, in the village of Tollard Royal.

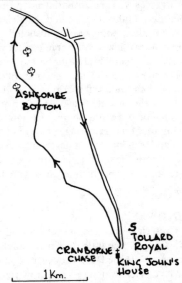

Cross the road to visit **Tollard Royal Church** and get a glimpse of **King John's House** behind it, then return to the pond and take the track to its left which leads away from the church.

At the first fork turn left, and follow the broad, grassy track which leads along the bottom of the valley. At the end of this valley, the ground drops away and opens out to left and right. Go through a gate and follow a track downhill as it bears left. Climb the stile shortly found on the right and bear right along the next valley floor. Keeping parallel with the fence on the left, head towards the wooded slope ahead. Climb the next stile and continue along the track beside the wood and past an abandoned cottage. At the next fork, turn left and continue to follow the grass track to the edge of a field in the valley bottom.

Skirt left round the edge of the field to reach the far left-hand corner, then take the small path leading away to the left. As the steep, grassy hillside opens out almost immediately to the right, make your way up it towards the belt of woodland above. The footpath through the trees has vanished completely, but the wood is not thickly overgrown and it is quite easy to make your way through the trees to the heath beyond. From here climb on up the steep hill, bearing right till you reach a gate in the fence. The views behind you as you climb are superb: on a clear day it is possible to see Bournemouth, the South Coast and, over to the left, the white cliffs of the Isle of Wight.

Go through the gate and turn right at the track. When you can see the road on your left near the track, continue to bear right along the track signed by-way to Tollard Royal. This brings you straight back to your starting point. As you near the village, look to your left for a view of Rushmore Lodge on the edge of **Cranbourne Chase** and, later, to your right for a fine view of the church.

POINTS OF INTEREST:

Tollard Royal Church – In the nave of the church is a 14th-century cross-legged effigy believed to be that of Sir William Payne. It is remarkable in being one of the few examples in which banded mail is represented. There is also a marble monument to General Pitt-Rivers, the archaeologist and ethnologist, who lived at nearby **Rushmore Lodge**, now a school.

King John's House – King John had a hunting lodge on the site now occupied by this fine Elizabethan manor house. It was later owned by General Pitt-Rivers.

Cranbourne Chase – Once a vast forest with a circumference of some 90 miles, Cranbourne Chase was a royal hunting ground from the time of King John to that of James I. By the 18th century, however, the forest had become something of a hideaway for poachers, smugglers, outlaws and vagabonds. Disputes and violence arose continually between these and the keepers of the forest, until finally, in 1830, Lord Rivers solved the problem by destroying large parts of the forest altogether, thus reducing it to manageable proportions. Small parts of the ancient woodlands still remain.

REFRESHMENTS:
Several in Tollard Royal.

GASPER MILL   5m (8km)

Maps: OS Sheets Landranger 183; Pathfinder ST 63/73.
Field paths, woodland tracks and green roads.
Start: The National Trust car park at Stourhead.

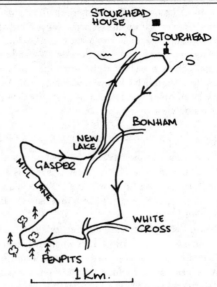

Walk with the Portakabin and a bench seat to the right. Where a wooden fence ends, left, turn left on to a path. Follow this and take a short grass track, left. Go through a gate, turn right and follow the fence. At the corner, ignore a gate ahead, turn left and follow the fence to a stile. Go over and turn right along the fence. Go through a gate in the right corner of the field and head towards farm buildings. To the right of these go through a gate and head for another gate in the fence, left. Go through and head for a gate in the fence, left, opposite a farmhouse. Go through on to a road. Turn right and walk down to a T-junction. Turn left, with **Bonham House** on your left, and almost immediately right into a green lane.

Follow the lane to reach a gate. Pass through, keeping close to the hedge on your right. Go through a further gate by a chalet house and continue on a surfaced road until a crossroads is reached. Go straight over and down a road to the hamlet of White Cross.

Just beyond White Cross Island bungalow at a T-junction, turn left and go down a steep hill until White Cross Cottage is reached. Turn left following a narrow steep road to Broadwater Farm. Fork left and continue to a stream. This is the 'stripling' River Stour. Follow the river and cross a wooden, white painted bridge. Go up a steep, often very muddy, track to the right. As you walk up through these woods you are passing through **Pen Pits**.

Ignore all turnings off the main track. At a T-junction (Pear Ash) turn right in front of a cottage. Pass between wooden posts. Here the track splits into two. Follow the right, descending track ignoring all tracks left and right. On reaching level ground a track from the left merges with your track, which bears to the right close to some tennis courts. Continue on the track to Gasper Corn Mill, now a private house. As you draw level with outbuildings, go through a wooden gate immediately to your left and walk close to a hedge along an ill-defined field path. This is Mill Lane. On reaching another gate, pass through on to a clearly defined track. At a T-junction turn right on to a metalled road and follow this through the tiny hamlet of Gasper. Eventually New Lake comes into view. Continue on up to a T-junction and turn left. Ignore a road climbing steeply to the right opposite a telephone kiosk and continue ahead with the lake down and left. After passing under an ornamental stone bridge you reach Stourhead. With the **Bristol Cross** on your left and St Peter's church to your right, go up the road and through a gate on the far side of the Spread Eagle Inn. Go through the inn yard and out through an archway on the left, through the inn car park and back into the main car park where you started the walk.

POINTS OF INTEREST:

Bonham House – The Chapel of St Benedict, long since deconsecrated, forms a part of this interesting building. After the Reformation it was a local centre for Catholicism.
The Bristol Cross – The medieval Bristol Cross stands at the entrance to the Gardens of Stourhead. It was moved to here in 1780.
Pen Pits – The hundreds of pits forming this complex of ancient stone quarries were in use long before the Norman Conquest. From them greensand stone was excavated to be fashioned into grinding and whetstones.

REFRESHMENTS:
The Spread Eagle Inn, Stourhead (tel no: 0747 840587).

Walk 82   SALISBURY PLAIN AND THE LAVINGTONS   5m (8km)
Maps: OS Sheets Landranger 173 & 184; Pathfinder SU 05/15.
An easy walk along part of the Salisbury Plain ridgeway.
Start: At 016544, a small car park by the stream in Market Lavington.

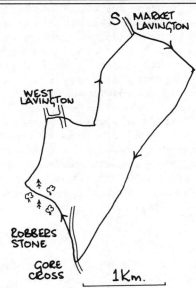

From the start continue along the metalled road, steadily ascending the northern scarp of Salisbury Plain. At the top turn right by the Ministry of Defence vedette. There is a metalled road along the line of the ridgeway, but the trackway immediately to the left provides more pleasant walking. Continue for about 2 miles. On reaching the farm buildings at St Joan a Gores Cross, fork right to reach the main Salisbury to Devizes road. Turn right along the road, looking out for the 'robbers stone' on the right, until a by-way sign on the left is reached in 150 yards. Turn left into a well-defined trackway, which descends steadily through woodland to an attractive stream with pond. The trackway now rises to a junction at which the lane on the right is followed down to **West Lavington**.

On reaching White Street turn right into Rickbarton and cross the main road. Bear

166

right into Rutts Lane, rising steadily along the metalled road. At a crossroads go straight across into a wooded trackway. On reaching a small clearing turn left and follow a narrow lane. The lane leads back to **Market Lavington** and the start. (The first part of this lane has been widened and given a rough surface for motor vehicles.)

POINTS OF INTEREST:
West Lavington – A large village straggling along the Salisbury to Devizes road. The fine clerestoried church holds much of interest.
Market Lavington – Former market town, now merely a large village.

REFRESHMENTS:
The Bridge Inn, West Lavington (tel no: 0380 813213).
The Kings Arms, Market Lavington (tel no: 0380 818429).
The Green Dragon, Market Lavington (tel no: 0380 813235).

Maps: OS Sheets Landranger 183; Pathfinder ST 84/94.
*A pleasant country ramble along woodland tracks and field
paths.*
Start: At 867414, the church in Longbridge Deverill.

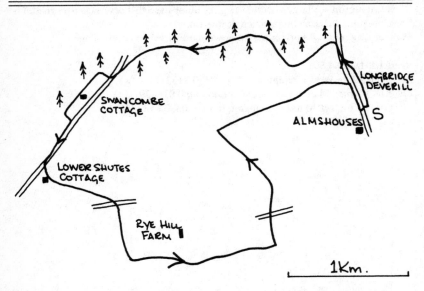

Go through a small wooden gate in the corner of the wall to the right of the lych gate.
Walk across the churchyard and go through a kissing gate and another gate a little way
ahead. Walk diagonally left across the field to a stile set in the wooden fence. Cross over
this stile and climb up the embankment by overgrown steps to reach the A350. Go over
with care, turn right and walk to a side road. Turn left and follow it to the edge of
woodland. Turn left here and keeping left follow the well-defined footpath until you
reach a fork. Take the left path and continue through the wood to a point where the path
again splits. Take the right-hand, narrow path and continue on to where another path
merges from the right. Do not follow the path directly ahead but bear left. After a short,
but steep, descent another path merges from the right and you bear left, following the
path on to a metalled road. Cross straight over and enter the gateway of Swancombe

cottage. Walk a short way up the drive and take a path on the left. Do not take the path going upwards, but walk parallel with the road you have just crossed. Follow the path until it brings you back on to the road again. Turn right and walk up the road until you reach Lower Shute cottage on your left.

Turn left through an entrance in front of the cottage, walk across a yard and go through a metal gate. Turn left and follow the hedge round the edge of this field to pass through another metal gate further along. Now ignore a wooden gate on your left and continue ahead until you reach a gate. Go through and cross a narrow, metalled road to reach a narrow track between tall hedges opposite. Follow this track down to a gate. Go through and walking diagonally left you will soon join a well-defined track. Turn left and walk along this track passing the house and outbuildings of Rye Hill Farm. Continue past the farm, following the track which soon broadens out. When you reach the point where the track turns sharply right take a narrower track that leads off left towards a modern bungalow. Follow this track to emerge on to a metalled road. Cross almost directly over the road on to another broad track and walk along this for some distance to a metal gate. Go through and continue to follow the track, dropping down into a dip and through another gate, until it brings you back out on to the A350. Cross over this very busy road, turn right and walk down the footpath until you reach the entrance to **Longbridge Deverill** church. Turn left and walk down through the churchyard until you reach the lych gate and the point from where you commenced the walk.

POINTS OF INTEREST:
Longbridge Deverill – The church has a small collection of ceremonial armour and an early art nouveau memorial. The Thynne Almhouses, built in 1655, are another interesting feature.

REFRESHMENTS:
The George, Longbridge Deverill (tel no: 0985 40396), serves bar snacks and meals. There are several cafés, restaurants and public houses in Warminster about 2 miles away.

Walk 84   WARDOUR WOODS AND CASTLE   5¹/₂m (9km)

Maps: OS Sheets Landranger 184; Pathfinder ST 82/92.

Field paths and woodland tracks in Nadder Valley.

Start: At 921253, the crossroads north-east of Donhead St Andrew.

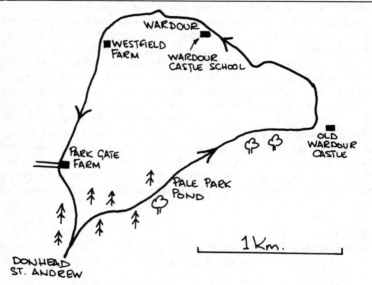

Walk up the No Through Road until a gate is reached, the entrance to Wardour Woods. Go through the opening left of the gate and up the track to where it bears right. Turn left on a path angled back left, and almost immediately right on to a narrow path. Go through a gate and across a field to a gate and stile. Go over and follow a path which skirts the edge of Pale Park pond. Continue through an opening keeping close to the fence, left. Go through another opening to reach a well-defined track. Follow this track with the wood on your right, going ahead at a point where it bears left. Continue instead along the grassy path to a large house and the boundary wall of **Wardour Castle**.

At a gate go through and walk up past a turning to the left which leads to Park Farm. Should you wish to visit the castle turn right across the car park. Otherwise climb over the wooden railed fence on your left into a field. Go diagonally across this field to pass just to the right of poultry houses. Continue diagonally across the field to reach the bottom right-hand corner. Turn left and follow the field edge until an opening is reached. Turn right and then right again on to a well-defined track. Follow this to a narrow road and the grounds of Wardour Castle Girls School. Follow the road, passing close to the school building, but at the point where it bears right, continue ahead on a rough path passing a hexagonal shaped house, left. Go over a cross-path and at a second cross-path turn left. Follow the path, passing to the right of three houses and through a sparse wood up to a staggered opening. Go through the opening into a field and walk diagonally left across it towards the red-tiled roof of Westfield Farm which soon comes into view. In the boundary fence to the right of the farm house there is a stile and another immediately opposite. Cross these and cross the field to an opening in a cross-fence. Go over two stiles close together and up to the edge of a wood.

With the wood and fence on your left continue until, close to Park Gate Farm, a line of trees is reached. Cross over the River Nadder by a rickety two-planked bridge. Cross the field to a gate. Go through, turn left and walk into the farmyard through a second gate. Turn right through a gap between the farm buildings to another gate. Walk a short distance into the field, then turn left and walk up the field to the top left-hand corner to pass through a narrow opening into a woodland clearing. Walk through the clearing to the top right-hand corner and turn right on to a well-defined path. Go through a gate and keeping close to the left-hand hedge walk to a stile. Cross over, turn right and walk back down the road to the crossroads from where you started the walk.

POINTS OF INTEREST:

Wardour Castle – Built in the 14th century by Lord Lovell, it subsequently became the home, for some 400 years, of the Arundell family, of whom Lady Blanche was the most famous. With a total compliment of around 29 souls she held out against a besieging force of 1,300 Parliamentarian troops for nearly ten days, before being forced to surrender. The castle is now administered by English Heritage and is open for most of the year.

REFRESHMENTS:

The Forrester, Donhead St Andrew (tel no: 074788 8122). Beer garden.

Walk 85   WHITESHEET HILL   6$\frac{1}{2}$m (10.5km)

Maps: OS Sheets Landranger 183; Pathfinder ST 63/73 & 83/93.

A walk on spectacular chalk downland.

Start: At 778342, the National Trust car park, Stourhead Gardens.

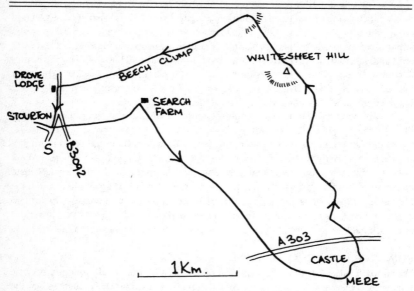

Leave the car park, turn right and walk back down the road to the T-junction with the
B3092. Cross over with care and take a lane almost opposite. Continue to Search Farm.
Follow the road in front of the farm buildings and ahead on a grass track in front of
yellow-painted cottages where the farm road turns right. Follow the path to a gate and
stile. Go over the stile and, keeping close to a hedge on your right, take a field path to
a gate. Go through and continue with a fence on your left. Cross a bridge over the A303
and bear slightly left to a gate and stile. Cross over and ascend the steep slope keeping
to the right of an electricity pole. Follow the path along the top of the ridge to a kissing
gate. Go through and on to a broad grassed area. Here there is a memorial stone to Sir
Winston Churchill and the high mound upon which **Mere Castle** once stood. To climb
the mound go down the steep path, ignore a set of steps going down to your right, follow
the path round and then climb a set of steps to the top. Your efforts will be rewarded

by superb views aided by an orientation table which will identify various landmarks for you.

Retrace your way to the point where you came to steps descending to your right. These are now to your left: go down them and follow a descending path down more sets of steps. Turn left and cross another bridge over the A303. At a track to the right (in front of a house and signposted to MOD Rifle Range) turn right, up a chalk track to reach a ridge of the downs. Continue to a gate to your left. Go through and continue upwards, shortly passing to the right of a tall transmitter aerial. In front of the main entrance to the site the track goes right and down to a cross track. Turn left along a broad chalk track which once formed a section of the Salisbury to West Country Coach Road. A little further on is a National Trust Information Board about **Whitesheet Hill** which you are now crossing. Further on is a stile, left, giving access to the National Trust site.

Continue on the track as it descends and turns left. Just beyond is a broad level area on your left often used as a car park. Turn left and walk diagonally to the far right-hand corner and take the descending path from there. This leads you down, then up through Beech Clump and finally down to reach the B3092 opposite Drove Lodge. With care, cross over the road, turn left and walk down to a narrow pathway leading off right. Take this path which soon brings you out by cottages to the road for Stourhead. Turn right for the NT car park start point.

POINTS OF INTEREST:

Mere Castle – The castle that used to top the mound was built in 1253 by Richard, Earl of Cornwall to protect the settlement of Mere. No trace of this fortress now remains. On top of the mound there is a memorial to the fallen of the 43rd Welsh Regiment, a replica of one erected outside Caen, Normandy.

Whitesheet Hill – Site of a hill fort which stood at the southern end. There are many interesting archaeological features, including evidence of a cross-ditch dyke and traces of an enclosed causeway dating from around 3000 BC.

REFRESHMENTS:

The Spread Eagle Inn , Stourhead (tel no: 0747 840587).

Walk 86   BIDCOMBE DOWN   6¹/₂m (10.5km)

Maps: OS Sheets Landranger 183; Pathfinder ST 83/93 & 84/94.
A scenic but isolated walk on ancient downland tracks.
Start: St Michael's Church, Brixton Deverill.

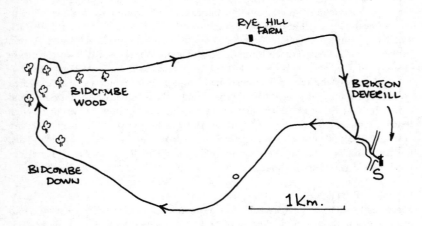

With the church behind you, walk back down the road to its junction with the B3095.
Turn right to reach River Dale cottage on your left. Here turn left and walk up a minor
road the metalled surface of which ends by the white Cliff House. Continue ahead on
a chalk track which, after passing farm buildings to the right, leads to a metal gate. Go
through, continue along the track. Just before a point where a line of trees and a fence
converge from the left, note a depression in the grass which is the remains of a dew-
pond. At the point where the fence ends and the track levels out before descending
steeply, turn left and walk up to a metal gate. Go through this and a second gate ahead.
Turn left immediately and follow the line of the fence as it climbs the field. Make for
a barn seen ahead shortly, to the right of which there is a gate and a ladder stile. Cross
the stile, and another one opposite, and follow distinct vehicle tracks up Cold Kitchen
Hill. The large, uncultivated mound to your right is a long barrow.

Shortly you will reach the OS Triangulation Pillar which marks the summit of Cold Kitchen at 845 feet. The views from here are superb. Continue to follow the vehicle track until a fence merges from the left. Follow the line of this fence until it makes a right-angled turn to the right. Here ignore the open gate and cross the fence. Keep another fence to your right and walk across the field to a metal gate. Go through the gate and continue along the fence, ignoring a further gate set in an angle. You are now on Bidcombe Down. Continue along the fence until it ends and a hedgerow begins. Here there is a crossing point. Cross the fence and pass through an opening immediately on your right. Turn left and follow a wire fence and shortly the edge of a wood until a gate is reached. Go through into the wood and follow the well-defined track which will take you to a height of 918 feet. Emerge from the wood and descend to a gate which leads into a field. Go through and turn immediately right. Keeping the line of Bidcombe Wood on your right, cross the field, bearing slightly right to reach two gates. Ignore the wooden gate leading into the wood and go through the metal gate. Turn right and follow the line of the wood for about $^1/_4$ mile, to another metal gate.

Go through the gate and continue to a further gate with a ladder stile. Climb over and follow a barbed wire fence for a short distance to another metal gate. Go through, turn left and walk to the bottom of the field. Turn right, keeping close to the left hedgerow which soon gives way to a wire fence. When you reach a wooden gate in this fence, bear across to the right on to a well-defined track. Follow this track, passing on your left the buildings and entrance to Rye Hill Farm. Here you enter a green lane. At a point where a narrow track leads off to a bungalow on the left and the broad track bears right, continue on the broad track which soon climbs up through the edge of a woodland and emerges on to a cross track. Turn left and follow the track to a road up which you previously walked by Cliff House at the start. Turn left and walk down on the road to a T-junction with the B3095. Turn right and walk back to the bridge over the River Wylye, where you turn left and walk back to the church.

REFRESHMENTS:
There are no refreshments in the immediate vicinity of this walk but the following nearby inn is close at hand:
The George, Longbridge Deverill (tel no: 0985 40396).

Walk 87   NORTH BRADLEY AND WEST ASHTON   6³/₄m (11km)

Maps: OS Sheets Landrangers 183 and 173; Pathfinder ST 85/95.
A mainly level walk through open countryside.
Start: At 854548, North Bradley Church.

Facing the church, turn left along the road, then, where it bends right, bear left of the tree on the green to reach a footpath, on the left signed 'Dursley 1/Westbury 3'. Turn left over a stile and bear right across two fields. Cross a stile at the far side and go along the left edge of the next field. Go through a gate at the far side and continue to reach a wide gap in the fence on the left. Go through and bear left to walk along the field edge, with a small stream on your left. At the far side, go through a gate on to a lane. Turn left across a ford and head up to Brook House Farm. There, bear left, right, then left again towards two barns. Just past the second barn, turn right and aim for the right edge of a copse ahead. At the far corner of the copse, bear left across a field, aiming to the left of a distant chimney. Go over a stile and along the edge of two fields to reach the road at Hawkeridge. Cross and go along the road opposite, passing the inn. At the road's end, ignore a path going left, continuing ahead over a stile. Maintain direction across

176

three fields to reach a track. Turn left to reach Hawkeridge Mill Kennels. Turn left, then right through a gate, go under a railway line and then bear slightly right for 150 yards. Now, at an earthbridge, on the right, turn left across a field, aiming to the left of Heywood Church. Cross a bridge and head towards a bungalow, going between it and a house to reach a road. Turn right to reach a road junction, with the church on your left.

Turn left along the A350 for 70 yards, then cross, with care, and go up the track signed for West Ashton. Go past Woodman's Cottage, on the left, and, after a further 200 yards, go over a gate. After 10 yards, turn right over a stile, then turn left and follow a field edge, then the edge of Clanger Wood. At a field corner, turn right for 40 yards, then turn left over a stile (NOT the one ahead of you) and bear left back towards the corner of the wood. Cross a footbridge and stile, then bear diagonally right across a field. Go through a gap and maintain direction across the next field to reach a double stile hidden in the hedge. Cross and go along the right edge of the next field. Just before the far corner, turn right over a stile and bear slightly left across a field to reach some houses and a road. Turn left for 150 yards, then left, through a gate, along a signed path for Yarnbrook. Bear left, go through a second gate, then bear left across a field to reach another gate, down in a small dip. Go through and, maintain direction to reach a stile in the hedge at the left edge of a small copse. Go straight across the next field and over a double stile. Now bear right towards the edge of a wood. Go over a stile in the corner, then turn right over a footbridge. Turn left along the wood's edge and, when the wood ends, go ahead across a paddock and through a garden enclosure to reach the A350 at Yarnbrook. Turn right for 120 yards, then cross, with care, and go down the track opposite, signed 'North Bradley 1'. Go over a stile and bear left across a field. In the opposite corner, turn left through a gate to reach the A363. Cross, with care, and turn right. About 20 yards after going under the railway, turn left on a path, signed for Dursley, which runs parallel to the railway. Turn right at the field corner: the River Biss is now on your left. Go along the riverbank to reach the second of two footbridges. Here, bear right to reach a stile in the far hedge. Cross and turn right towards **North Bradley Church**. Go over a stile and along an enclosed path to reach a small housing estate. Turn left to reach the main road and turn left again to reach the church.

POINTS OF INTEREST:
North Bradley Church - Dedicated to St Nicholas, the church has a list of incumbents dating back to 1316. The chalice and paten are 14th-century.

REFRESHMENTS:
The Royal Oak, Hawkeridge.
The Long Arms, Yarnbrook.

Walk 88   BRATTON AND EDINGTON   6³/₄m (11km)

Maps: OS Sheets Landranger 183 & 184; Pathfinder ST 85/95.

A walk with a steep climb, but with magnificent views.

Start: The Duke Hotel, or also the car park behind Jubilee Hall opposite, Bratton.

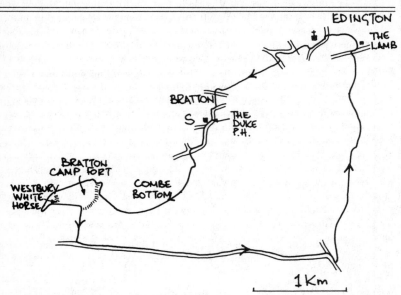

Walk along the main road with The Duke on your right and take the second turning on the left (The Butts). At the top, by the old school, bear right. When the road starts to dip take the footpath on the left to St James' Church. At the church gate take the path on the right and go over a stile. Bear left past trees and gradually climb to the fence at the top. Follow on with the fence on your left, cross over a stile and continue with the fence on your right. Turn right through a gate and go along a sunken track. At the head of the valley (known as Combe Bottom) climb the grass bank and make towards the road. Cross over and continue round the edge of the earth mound of **Bratton Castle Hill Fort.**

Follow the path until you come to a stone plinth and panorama dial and **Westbury White Horse**. Walk back towards the horse and then follow a track to the top of the outer mound and on to a road. Turn right and walk towards a barn. Turn left round the barn and follow the track for about $1^1/_2$ miles. All the land to your right belongs to the army. Keep out! Turn right towards an army post at a road junction, then double back to your left along a grass track. Follow this track, which bears right, until you come to a barn. Turn right, then left, round the barn and go through two gates. Continue on through two more gates. Bear right after the second gate to another gate beyond which go down a gully to a main road (B3098). Turn right along the road and after about 50 yards cross over to a stile on the left. You will see The Lamb ahead of you if you need a rest. Otherwise go over the stile and follow the hedgerow on the right until you come to a small wooden gate leading on to a road. Turn left passing houses on your left. Turn left at a road junction and follow the wall on the right to **Edington Priory Church**.

Enter the churchyard and take a path to the left and go through a gate. The path leads to a road. Turn left, then first right and right again to walk past the Old Manor Farmhouse on your left. Take the first turning on the left (Greater Lane) and about 30 yards up, go over a stile on the right signposted to Bratton. Go over another stile, up a bank and continue with the hedgerow on your right over two more stiles. The path now leads down to a stream. Turn right, then left across the stream passing in front of a house. Cross the road and follow the path opposite which leads to the centre of Bratton, the Duke Hotel and the start.

POINTS OF INTEREST:

Bratton Castle Hill Fort – Dates from the Iron Age.

Westbury White Horse – The oldest of many in Wiltshire, but has been re-modelled several times. Cut in 1778, but there was a much older one on this hill at that time.

Edington Priory Church – To St Mary, St Katharine and All Saints. Dates from 1352. The clock, which has no dial, is one of the oldest working clocks in the country.

REFRESHMENTS:

The Duke , Bratton (tel no: 0380 830242), with garden.

The Lamb, Edington (tel no: 0380 830263), pub with garden.

Walk 89   **SHASTON DROVE**   7m (11km)

Maps: OS Landranger Sheet 184; Pathfinder Sheet ST 82/92.

Field paths, tracks and an ancient drove road. Dogs must be on leads.

Start: The church at Alvediston.

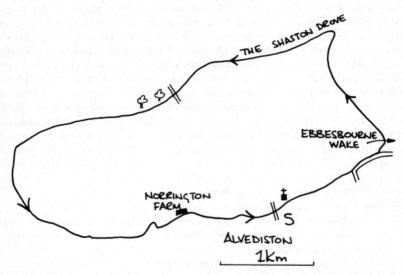

With the church and the old Rectory on your left, walk down the field to a gate. Go through and walk ahead to another gate. Go through and walk down a narrow path between cottages until you reach a metalled road. Turn left and follow the road up and round for about $1/4$ mile. Keep a sharp look out for a wooden gate on top of the banking to your left and a bridleway sign. Climb the bank and go through the gate, turning immediately right. Keep walking parallel to the wire fence on your right, following it round and up the field to reach a metal gate. Go through and continue walking with the fence on your right until you come to a stile. Cross over and continue along the almost overgrown path to a ladder stile. Cross this and join a well-defined path merging from the left. Turn right and follow this path until a cross track is reached. Here, turn left. You are now on the Shaston Drove.

Follow the drove road, at one point crossing over a metalled road, until you reach the second of two conifer plantations. About 120 yards further on turn left on to a footpath descending between high banks. Follow this path down and round to a small wooden gate. Go through the gate and walk down through an opening, turning immediately left to cross over a low railed section of fence on to a well-defined track. Turn right and follow this track to a metal gate. Go through the gate and keeping close to the fence and hedge on your right, follow it down to a point where it makes a right-angled turn to the right. Here take a diagonal line across to your left until a cross fence is reached. Turn left and follow this fence down to a point where a track merges from the left and there is an open gateway in front of you. Walk straight ahead down the farm road until you reach a line of beech trees on your right. Here there is a stile. Cross it and turn diagonally left across the field to pass just to the right of Norrington Farm, the roof of which can be seen above the trees. On reaching a metal gate go through on to a farm road. Turn left and follow the road round to the right to another metal gate. Go through and, keeping parallel to the wire fence on your left, follow it until it borders the garden of a cottage. Here you will find a stile in the fence. Cross it into the garden of the cottage. Turn immediately right and walk down to a metalled road. Turn right, and almost immediately left, to take a footpath which leads down to a wooden gate. Go through the gate and walk across the short meadow to reach a stile. Cross over the stile on to a metalled road. Almost opposite is the entrance into the meadow which will lead you back to the church from where you started the walk.

POINTS OF INTEREST:
Apart from the superb scenery throughout this walk, there are several tumuli and other earthworks to be identified.
St Mary's, Alvediston – The tomb of Sir Anthony Eden, Prime Minister from 1955-1957, lies in the churchyard.

REFRESHMENTS:
The Crown, Alvediston (tel no: 0722 780335).

Maps: OS Sheets Landranger 184; Pathfinder ST 84/94.
A fairly strenuous walk to Middle Hill.
Start: At St Aldhelm's church, Bishopstrow.

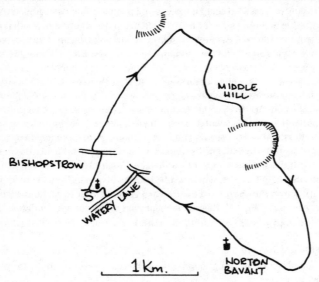

With the church to your right walk down the road to a kissing gate. Go through and follow the path through another gate and over a river bridge to emerge on to the B3414 (A36). Cross over, turn left and walk down the footpath until you reach an opening to your right. Turn right here and follow the track past a farmhouse and outbuildings, over a railway bridge and up to a point where the fence on your right ends by a stile. Turn right and follow the well-defined path across a field to reach an opening which leads directly on to a metalled road. Cross the road and go through the opening opposite. Turn right immediately and follow the path, by a hedge, until a cross fence is reached. Do not go through the opening in this fence, but turn left and follow the path and the fence as it climbs up **Middle Hill.**

   It turns sharply and leads to a stile. Cross over, turn left and walk a short distance up the narrow track to reach an opening on your right. Go through on to a metalled road which leads down to North Farm. Walk a short distance towards the farm crossing over a stile on your right which leads directly up the short field to another stile. Cross over, turn left and walk parallel with the fence on your left until you are opposite North Farm down on the left. Here, take a diagonal line right, up the hill towards a cross fence. With this fence to your left continue to follow the path up the east side of Middle Hill passing through a gap by a now defunct stile. Continue along this path as it descends, turning through a right-angle left, until you a see a cross fence down to your right. Walk down to this fence. Do not go through the gap, but turn left, and keeping the fence on your right follow it to a gate. Go through to reach the B3414 at its junction with the new roundabout to the west of Heytesbury.

With care, cross over this junction and take the B3095. Cross over the railway bridge and immediately turn right down a steep, railed path. At the bottom, do not go through the metal gate on to railway property, but turn left, cross over the fence and take a diagonal line across a field to a gate in the top left-hand corner. Go through and walk ahead towards cottages. By the cottages climb over a stile on to a metalled road and enter the village of Norton Bavant. Follow the road, ignoring a turning left, down to a T-junction. Cross to reach a driveway and follow this down to another T-junction. Again cross over, into a field. Turn left, then right over a culvert. Follow the field path until you reach a cottage where you will need to cross over to your right, taking a path which leads past it. Do not follow right the service road to the cottage, but cross into a field and walk diagonally towards the top right-hand corner. Here turn left into Watery Lane and follow it to a stile in the hedge, right, just beyond the Trout Farm. Cross over and follow the path through a kissing gate back to St Aldhelm's church.

POINTS OF INTEREST:

Middle Hill – Once overshadowed the ancient settlement of Middleton, of which no trace now exists. The Iron Age hill forts of Battlesbury and Scratchbury which seemingly buttress the south-western escarpment of Salisbury Plain are a dominating feature of the area. Several paths lead off the main walk route to enable the walker to visit either of the two forts, from which vantage points there are superb views over the Wylye Valley and the Plain of Warminster.

Walk 91 BROAD CHALKE AND THE EBBLE VALLEY 7½m (12km)

Maps: OS Sheets Landranger 184; Pathfinder SU 02/12.

A combination of valley and downland in a very pretty part of the country.

Start: The United Reformed Church in Broad Chalke.

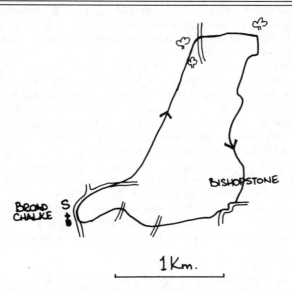

Turn left just past the telephone box up the footpath along the side of the churchyard. Turn right on to a tarmac road which comes to an end in a cottage garden. The road now becomes a footpath and you are out of the village into countryside. At the second gate keep to the edge of the field before dropping down to a concrete farm road where you turn left up the hill. This takes you into a valley. Pass farm buildings to where the path forks. Take the right fork and follow the Right of Way across an open field heading for the left of the wood. At the wood, do not follow the main track to the right but keep to the edge of the wood for 30 yards to where the path turns into the wood. You will meet a metalled track which you follow to the cross tracks at the edge of the wood. Turn right. (If you carry straight on for 100 yards to the brow of the hill you will get a fine view to the north west over the Nadder Valley.) Just over ½ mile further, having passed a barn on your right, you come to another crossways where you turn right down the hill to Bishopstone. Turn right on to the main road in Bishopstone and then left just in front of the pub. Follow the road through the village and when you swing right by the River Ebble you will see the Three Horse Shoes Inn, a charming unspoilt pub that sells Wadworth beer and sandwiches.

The final part of the walk, about $1^3/_4$ miles, is along a poorly-kept Right of Way that keeps near the river bank to Broad Chalke. Take the road for Croucheston Mill, cross the river by the watercress beds and 100 yards from the bridge turn right at the crossroads. Turn right again at the T-junction. Go through the farmyard and out on to a track beyond. The Right of Way, which is not clear, keeps to the hedge. There is now a short piece of road past Leyton Manor. Immediately you will see a track forking right, which you follow between the farmyard and the water mill. Note the old granaries on their staddle-stones. The Right of Way now keeps to the river and although it is overgrown there are stiles. There is one road to cross before you go over a big field and come into the southern end of Broad Chalke close to a farm. Turn right down the road, keeping the church on your left and you will arrive back in the centre of Broad Chalke by the Queens Head Inn.

REFRESHMENTS:
The Queens Head Inn, Broad Chalke (tel no: 0722 780344).
The Three Horse Shoes Inn, Bishopstone (tel no: 0722 780491).

Walk 92   AROUND SUTTON VENY   10m (16km)

Maps:OS Sheets Landranger 183 & 184; Pathfinder ST 83/93 and ST 84/94.

Along ancient trackways over high, remote chalk downlands.
Start: At 902417, the car park by the church, Sutton Veny.

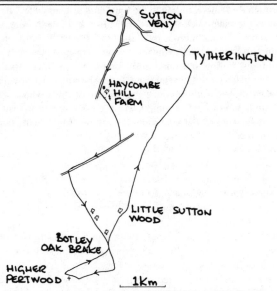

Turn right out of the car park. At a crossroads turn left into Hill Road and follow it up on to the downs. After passing Haycombe Hill Farm, left, the road bears round to the left beside a barn where the metalled surface ends. Continue along a broad, well-defined but rough track. At a cross track turn right and go down towards the A350 and Lords Hill. At the next cross track turn left along a grassy track between tall hedges. At the apex of Botley Oak Brake another track merges from the left. Continue on until a Dutch barn is reached. There turn right and walk up a path close to the right-hand hedge. Shortly you will reach the hamlet of **Higher Pertwood**.

Passing between two small, neat greens, bear right in front of the Manor House, then turn left between two brick gate posts and walk towards a barn. On the left you will see the ruined Church of St Peter. *Do not enter*. Retrace your steps back to the road and turn left. At the junction a few yards up the road turn left and walk through an avenue of tall trees. At the end turn right immediately on to a waymarked field path. Follow this, keeping close to the right-hand fence, to emerge on to a track walked previously. Here turn left and walk back to Botley Oak Brake where the tracks divide. Take the extreme right track close to the hedge. Ignore a path going off left through Little Sutton Woods, and continue through two wooden gate posts on to a broad chalk track. Follow this down through Redding Hanging to the bottom of a steep valley. Pass through two gates and follow the steep track up out of the valley, passing through another gate by a Dutch barn, where a track merges from the left.

Continue to follow the track to the point where it turns sharply left in front of a gate and farm buildings. Follow it around and continue to the Wylye Valley road at the western end of Tytherington. Turn right and walk a short distance down the road to visit the **Church of St James**. Retrace your steps back up the road. Those who wish to visit the ruined Church of St Leonard should take a grass track on the right opposite the Sutton Veny village sign. Otherwise continue walking down the road until the village and car park are reached.

To return to Sutton Veny from St Leonard's Church, either retrace your steps back to the valley road or negotiate the simple wooden fence at the western end of the churchyard, follow the short grassed path down to a road, turn left and walk up to where it joins the valley road where you turn right and on to the car park.

POINTS OF INTEREST:

Higher Pertwood – The present Manor House stands in this tiny hamlet on the site of a former farm house built well before the Norman Conquest. It was built in the 18th century, but has been extensively altered. St Peter's Church was also built during the 18th century but a church has existed on this site since 1332. St Peter's was declared redundant in 1972 and sold. Its bell cote, now empty, once housed the oldest bell in Wiltshire. *Do not attempt to enter, the building is now derelict.*

St James' Church ,Tytherington – Reputed to be the oldest church in Wiltshire.

REFRESHMENTS:

The Woolpack, Sutton Veny (tel no: 0985 40422).

Walk 93   **KINGSTON DEVERILL**   10m (16km)

Maps: OS Sheets Landranger 183; Pathfinder ST 83/93.

A delightful downland walk mainly on field paths and green lanes.

Start: Kingston Deverill Church.

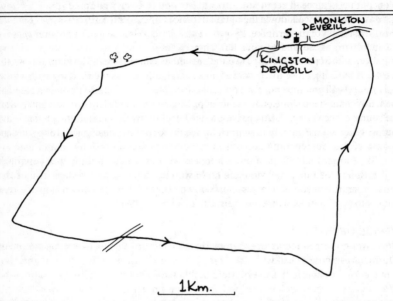

Leave the church on your right and walk down the road to the point where it turns right: a driveway leads off to the left and there is a No Through road opposite. Cross the road and walk up the No Through Road for a short distance until an opening on the left is reached which leads up to a dairy. Turn left and then pass through a gate immediately on the right , beside which there is a bridleway sign to Whitesheet Hill. Cross the small field diagonally up to the top left-hand corner. Go through a gate and through another gate immediately opposite. Take a diagonal line to the right and walk up the sloping field until you reach the corner of a wire fence. Turn left and follow the line of this fence until it veers away left. Continue to walk straight ahead following a well-defined path until a gate is reached. Go through this gate and continue until you come alongside another fence on your left. Follow this fence for a little over $^1/_2$ mile until it takes a right-angled turn right where there is a small wooden gate in the corner. Turn left and go through the gate. Follow a fence on your right until a metal gate is reached. Turn right through this gate and cross the field directly to another gate ahead. Go through and continue with a wire fence on your left until you reach a small wooden gate. Go through this gate and still walking straight ahead continue until a metal gate is reached which leads out on to a broad green lane, the old London to Exeter turnpike.

Turn left and walk down the old road to the B3095. With care, cross over to reach a further section of the turnpike. Pass through a series of metal gates until you come to a Dutch barn ahead and to your left, shortly before the A303. Here there are two entrances into separate fields. Take the second entrance on your left and follow the well-defined path, close to a fence, as it rises and falls across the field to reach a gate. Go through and continue until a cross fence and gate is reached. Go through a gate and walk down the steep slope on to the floor of a narrow valley. Here turn left and follow the course of the valley, shortly passing to the left of two trees. Bear slightly left to reach a cross fence with a gate up to your right. Go through this gate and still following the course of the valley, continue until farm buildings and a cross fence and gate are reached. Go through the gate on to a narrow metalled lane. Follow this down to a T-junction in the village of Monkton Deverill. Turn left and walk a short distance up the road until you come to its junction with the B3095. Turn left and follow the road back into Kingston Deverill and the start.

REFRESHMENTS:

There are no refreshments in the immediate vicinity of this walk but the following nearby inn is close at hand:

The George, Longbridge Deverill (tel no: 0985 40396).

Walk 94   **THE WINTERBOURNES**   3m (5km)

Maps: OS Sheets Landranger 184; Pathfinder SU 03/13.

A gentle stroll in the valley of the River Bourne.

Start: At 175344, a lay-by south of Winterbourne Earls church.

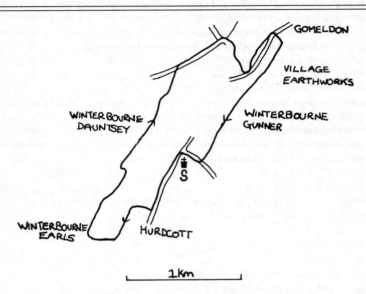

Walk along the roadside for about $\frac{1}{2}$ mile and, where the pavement ends, turn right through a small gate, following a signpost to Hurdcott. At the end of this track there is a gate. Go through and turn left along the road and then into a track on the right as the road bends left. Pass a small pumping station, cross the River Bourne and, at the entrance to a small works, take a narrow path to the right. Almost immediately turn right again, over a stile and continue along the edge of a field. On reaching a metalled road, carry on, taking a wide track ahead in 50 yards. At the next metalled road, turn left for 60 yards, and go through a gap in the hedge on the right. Carry straight on over two more stiles. Cross another metalled road, and then follow a track along the hedge line on the right of the field. As the field boundary bends left, go over a stile on the right. Proceed diagonally across a small field to a stile leading to the main road. Turn right along the road and right again at the roundabout into **Winterbourne Gunner**.

Note the decorated gate of a house called Brooklands, on the left immediately before a grassy track which leads to the very attractive small church. Turn left at the road junction and then left over a stile to follow a field path towards Comeldon, the site of a medieval village. Rejoin the road over a stile and, in 100 yards, turn right down a few steps. Go through a small gate and follow a path bending gradually to the right. Carry on through gaps in the hedges and then follow a generally straight line for almost 1 mile, passing through a residential area on the way. At the second metalled road turn right to return to the main road at **Winterbourne Earls** church. The starting point is a short distance to the left.

POINTS OF INTEREST:
Winterbourne Gunner – Has a well-situated, largely 13th-century church, with a Norman tower.
Winterbourne Earls – The 19th-century church was built by Wyatt to replace demolished churches at Winterbourne Earls and Winterbourne Dauntsey, re-using materials from both medieval buildings.

REFRESHMENTS:
The Tything Mann Inn, Winterbourne Dauntsey (tel no: 0980 611306).

NEAR THE RIVER AVON   4m (6.5km)

Maps: OS Sheets Landranger 184; Pathfinder SU 03/13.

An easy walk through rich water meadows with fine views over Salisbury Plain.

Start: At 126353, on the road at the north end of Lower Woodford.

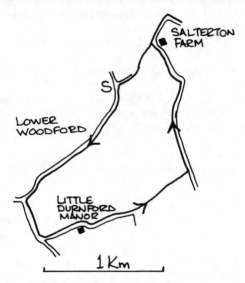

Go south through the village and follow the road to a junction on your left. Little Durnford Manor is to the left here. Turn left down a private road through the estate. You will eventually emerge through a door in a wall on to a road. Cross the road and continue up the lane by a wood. Turn left at the crossroads by a thatched cottage. The road becomes a track and you continue along this to a copse.

Go through a gate at the edge of the copse and cross the edge of a field, keeping the fence on your left. At the end of the field there is a barbed wire gate which can be opened with a wire loop. Go through and turn left. Go down the track through a farmyard and on to the road. Turn left and then immediately right down a lane. This turns into a footpath and crosses two bridges on the way back to Lower Woodford and the starting point.

REFRESHMENTS:
Several in Lower Woodford.

Walk 96   CHUTE CAUSEWAY   4¹/₂m (7.5km)

Maps: OS Sheets Landranger 174 & 185; Pathfinder SU 25/35.
Along quiet lanes with fine views and woodland pathways.
Start: The church in Upper Chute.

Walk up the hill for about ¹/₂ mile, looking back for a good view of the church and the rolling countryside behind as you near the top of the ridge. At the farm on the right bear left along a track between two fences. On reaching the road, turn left. This straight road along the top of the ridge is **Chute Causeway** and the views into the valley on the right are superb.

   Walk along the causeway for about 1 mile until you reach a wide gravel track on the left, signposted to Rushford's Stud. Take the first stony track on the right towards the farm buildings (called New Zealand!). At the end of the field on the left follow a track between trees, rejoining Chantry Lane near a small white bungalow on the right. Continue straight on down the gravel track beneath trees and, after passing the stud, turn right in front of the metal gate straight ahead. Go through a gate and continue on up the hill, bearing left under trees as you near the top. Go through the gate straight

194

ahead and bear slightly right across the field, making for the gate on the opposite side beyond the clumps of trees. Here you will find yourself walking along the course of an ancient earthwork which leads to the gate. Follow the grassy track on the line of the ancient ditch into woodland. Where the main track forks, take the left fork and turn left at the first crossroads. When you come to the broad track leading past a cottage on the right, follow it past the cottage and bear right into the field beyond. Follow the track up the hill, passing a bungalow on your left, and turn right at the road near the Cross Keys pub. As you come into the village, take the first turning on the left beside a grass triangle and continue in the same direction along other small lanes until you reach the church once more.

POINTS OF INTEREST:

Chute Causeway – This follows the course of an old Roman Road and joins typically straight roads leading north and south. It is, in fact, part of a whole network of Roman roads which criss-cross Wiltshire. Routes between London, Bath, Cirencester and Winchester (all important Roman towns) passed through the county. Nearby Biddesden House is on the site of a Roman villa.

REFRESHMENTS:
Available in Upper Chute.

Walk 97 LUDGERSHALL CASTLE AND COLLINGBOURNE WOOD

5m (8km)

Maps: OS Sheets Landranger 184; Pathfinder SU 25/35.

Mainly on well-marked woodland paths. A small part lies through Ministry of Defence property, where dogs must be kept on leads.

Start: At 264511, the car park near Ludgershall Castle.

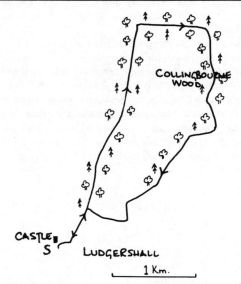

Follow the road past the castle, away from the town, and continue to a field. Turn left inside the field and follow the path along the left-hand fence to a stile. Head straight on along the gravel track which leads past a farm and into **Collingbourne Wood.** Keep to the track for about 1 mile, then, as the track drops downhill and veers to the right, continue straight on down a smaller path between the trees. When you meet the gravelled road which leads from the right-hand side, turn left on to it, then almost immediately, turn right along a grassy track which continues through the wood. At the end of this track, go through a gate and continue in the same direction, down the left-hand side of a field. Turn right in the valley bottom and cross a field to a gate on the far side. Follow the track which leads along the valley bottom and back into the wood.

196

At the point where a broad gravel track cuts across your path, continue straight on, bearing right at the edge of a wood. Go through the first gateway on the left, and continue in the same direction along the track which leads round the edge of the wood. After passing through two fields the track leads between the wood and a hedge on the left. Follow the line of the left-hand hedge and then bear left down a track between a small coppice and a hedge on the right. As you reach the road turn immediately right, down a track which leads along the edge of the first field you crossed. Find a stile on the left at the far end of the field and retrace your steps back to **Ludgershall Castle.**

POINTS OF INTEREST:

Collingbourne Wood – Probably this was once part of the great Chute Forest which stretched from Savernake into Hampshire. A royal forest, it was kept well stocked with deer and in the rein of Henry III red deer were sent to royal favourites or to furnish the royal table.

Ludgershall Castle – There is little left of the castle except the grass grown ditches and some ruined stonework. It is thought to have been built at some time during the late 11th century and was used as a hunting lodge by Henry III in the 13th century. The castle fell into decay around the 15th and 16th centuries. The surrounding ramparts, once fortified with wooden palisades, are extensive enough to give some idea of large and impressive defences.

Walk 98   OLD SARUM AND LOWER WOODFORD   5m (8km)
Maps: OS Sheets Landranger 184; Pathfinder SU 03/13.
An easy walk along the Woodford Valley.
Start: The car park at Old Sarum.

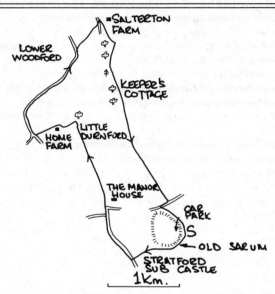

Walk back along the entrance road a short distance then turn right along a chalky path. Before reaching the main road, turn right and follow a signposted bridleway to the pleasant village of **Stratford sub Castle.** At a junction of paths in 200 yards, bear right again. On reaching the metalled road, turn right along the roadside footway, passing the church on the right. Do not cross the river, but continue along Phillips Lane with the manor house on the right, until Little Durnford is reached. Upon reaching woodland, look out for a gatehouse on the left, opposite a post box. Follow a footpath sign through a latched door, along a wide avenue to Home Farm and a bridge over the River Avon. At the next crossroads turn right along the road signposted 'Amesbury'. Lower Woodford is reached in $^{3}/_{4}$ mile. Go through the village. After passing a telephone box on the right, turn right into the next driveway. Keep left and follow a narrow tarmac pathway to three footbridges crossing the river. The route continues uphill to reach the road. Turn left along the road for 30 yards and turn sharply right into Salterton Farm. Pass through two farmyard gates and continue through a field to the upper left-hand corner. Bear slightly left and almost immediately turn right along a track to Keeper's Cottage. Return to Old Sarum along a well-defined lane. Just short of Old Sarum, turn right for a short distance on a metalled road before taking a path on the left which leads round to the **Old Sarum** access road.

POINTS OF INTEREST:
Lower Woodford, Stratford sub Castle – Very attractive thatched villages. The church at Stratford sub Castle has a particularly attractive interior.
Old Sarum – The original Salisbury. Prehistoric site, Iron Age hill fort and Roman Sorviodunum. Later occupied by the Saxons.

REFRESHMENTS:
The Old Castle Inn , adjacent to Old Sarum (tel no: 0722 28703).
The Wheatsheaf, Lower Woodford (tel no: 072273 203).

Walk 99   UPAVON AND NORTH NEWNTON   7m (11km)

Maps: OS Sheets Landranger 173 & 184; Pathfinder SU 05/15.

A walk combining part of the Avon valley with the Salisbury Plain ridgeway.

Start: The public conveniences, Upavon village.

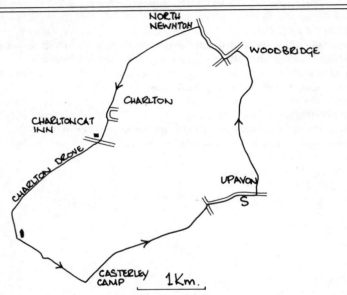

Proceed along the side of the main road towards Andover, crossing the river. Turn left into a metalled road, posted as a cul-de-sac. Pass farm buildings on the left as the road becomes an unsurfaced lane. The route is quite straightforward, following the course of the river. On reaching a junction of paths bear left. On reaching the main road, turn left, and cross the river to reach the Woodbridge Inn. Turn right at the telephone box and follow the metalled road towards **North Newnton**.

On reaching a farm, turn left, between the two large buildings. North Newnton church can be visited by a short diversion to the right. Follow the gently rising unsurfaced lane towards Wilsford. As the main track swings to the right, turn left into a lesser track, opposite a sign warning that dogs must be kept under control. In 50 yards the track divides again: take the left fork towards **Charlton**.

At first the way is a little overgrown, but it soon improves. On reaching a metalled road in Charlton hamlet, proceed straight ahead, shortly leaving the road to pass a farm on a track which reaches the main road beside the Charlton Cat Inn. Cross the road and follow a wooded track rising quite steeply. An unsurfaced roadway joins on the left and you are soon in open country, climbing steadily past the edge of a belt of trees towards the plateau of Salisbury Plain. On meeting the major Ridgeway track turn left, reaching Casterley vedette in $^3/_4$ mile. Turn left into a metalled road, noting the earthwork of Casterley Camp on the right. Views from this elevated section of roadway include the North Wessex Downs, with the Alton White Horse (see Walk 78) prominent. **Upavon** is reached in $1^1/_2$ miles.

POINTS OF INTEREST:
North Newnton – With a simple church near the river, close to a mill.
Charlton – Small hamlet. Church has perpendicular tower and chapel, but is otherwise Victorian. Birthplace of Stephen Duck, the 'thresher poet'.
Upavon – Large busy village with shops, thatched cottages and church with a 13th-century tower.

REFRESHMENTS:
The Woodbridge Inn (tel no: 0980 630266).
The Ship Inn, Upavon (tel no: 0980 630313).

Maps: OS Sheets Landranger 184; Pathfinder SU 03/13.
A walk over a hilly area, very much for those who enjoy woodland.
Start: The Royal Oak, Great Wishford.

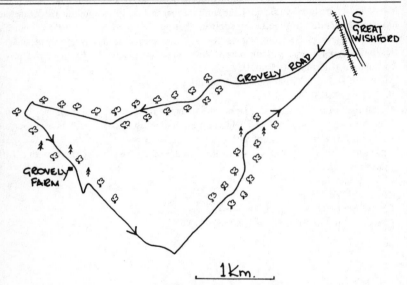

From the road junction by the inn, proceed under the railway and follow the metalled Grovely road, initially in open country, eventually entering woodland. The road rises steadily until a junction with a track on the line of a Roman road is reached. Turn right and follow this straight track, now a bridleway, for ^{1}/$_2$ mile. Through the woodland to the left, a large open area is apparent. On reaching the end of this open area, turn left and, shortly, left again at a junction of tracks. In ^{1}/$_2$ mile, note a pair of derelict cottages on the right and carry on past Grovely Farm. In 400 yards, turn sharp left at a small pit, followed by a sharp right turn 150 yards further on. The track emerges from the wood and descends to join the Ox Drove. An old milestone on the left marks a left turn. Ascend steadily back toward the woodland, pass plantations of young trees and cross the trackway which is on the line of the Roman road. A pleasantly undulating track carries on, firstly through woodland, then emerging on to open hillside with long and wide views over the Wylie Valley during the descent to **Great Wishford**. Pass under the railway and turn left to return to the main part of the village.

POINTS OF INTEREST:

Great Wishford – A well situated village off the busy A36 road. The church was substantially restored in 1863/4. Other interesting buildings include the Grobham almshouses (1628) and the Howe school.

REFRESHMENTS:

The Swan Inn, Stoford (tel no: 0722 790236).
The Royal Oak Inn, Great Wishford (tel no: 0722 790229).

TITLES IN THE SERIES